Orleath

THE

COLIVING

CODE

Shark Tank 😊
Power

Christine McDannell

Foreword

As someone who has worked tirelessly to build a brand worth being proud of, I'm no stranger to the feeling of fierce motivation and passion for a vision. This core ambition is something I share with Christine, with whom I was able to personally spend time with and explore these ideas together. She told me about the innovative ways in which she hopes to reimagine living spaces and create a sense of comradery, luxury and efficiency by sharing resources throughout these homes with her current venture, Kindred Quarters. Christine is someone who works tirelessly on giving back and helping others. It's refreshing to be around such a passionate and talented entrepreneur working on making this world a better place.

As a serial entrepreneur, she has already made some fantastic strides with eight successful companies under her belt. Her experience and ambition have allowed her to think outside the box and refuse to back down. I was fascinated by her commitment to turn the real estate industry on its head and develop solutions to a widespread problem as opposed to mere ways of coping. Instead of accepting that housing is becoming scarce in space and increasingly costly, she decided to create an answer that solves multiple pains at once. These core elements of community and sharing of resources are not only key to a fulfilling life, but also to any thriving business.

For these reasons, I'm delighted to introduce the content you're about to dive into. When a seemingly impossible challenge presents itself, I am a proponent of always pushing harder and reaffirming the commitment to succeed. The harder a problem appears, the more exciting it will be to solve. That's why the fantastic tools you're about to learn will serve you in countless corners of your life. So prepare to view things in a new way, because once you take these ideas in, there's no turning back.

-Richard Branson

Table of Contents

Introduction

Welcome to the age of disruption. Every major industry is in the process of serious overhauls. From shared cars (Uber, TURO), shared homes (Airbnb), to filling extra space in your suitcase by transporting items for others, the world has finally begun to take advantage of surplus space and resources through the rise of the **sharing economy**.

Coliving is a global movement that's shaping the future of how we live. It's a way for a group of people to join together to live in a beautiful place and share common resources that they might not be able to access otherwise.

It's time to learn about the shift that's redefining the term 'roommate' with something meaningful, sustainable, creative, and healthy. We'll discuss different coliving options with experts and founders of this new movement. These people will help to develop what coliving looks like over the next few years and beyond.

This innovative approach to modern residence models is challenging the housing problems we face in big cities. By taking advantage of large houses and lonely millennials, coliving has become the newest disruption of surplus space.

Coliving, at its core, is making best use of resources and space that typically do not get maximum usage, such as joint kitchens and central recreation spaces, shared amenities, more residents than an average housing situation, and the presence of a coworking area.

Additionally, coliving homes offer more flexible short-term lease options: nightly, weekly, and monthly. This provides freedom and mobility, especially to a current generation of people who appreciate a lesser degree of commitment and love to travel.

As the founder of Kindred Quarters, I'm excited to help you take a deep look at the new industry of coliving: the past, present, and future. I have a drive to help educate others about this exciting industry and this book is the perfect means to do so.

Whether you've considered living in a coliving space or have never heard the term before, this book will give you the information you need to understand this new movement in the housing industry and even help you start your own home.

There are so many benefits to sharing living space that it's amazing that it hasn't been done at scale before. Of course, technology has helped us in this respect. Advances in the way we communicate and how we organize our lives have helped the coliving initiative take hold. There are so many ways in which you can take advantage of the current and future tech to make life easier. Coliving is an important one of these that deserves to be explored in more detail.

One

Innovation

What is Currently Happening

Times are definitely changing. It takes just three clicks to book a place to stay on Airbnb. On the other hand, it could take three weeks to secure an apartment using standard leasing procedures, if not longer. Looks like it is due time that **HaaS** (Housing as a Service) disrupts the antiquated industry of property management and real estate. In fact, it's already beginning to happen. With the rise of recent coliving companies like The Collective in the UK (which is expanding into the US soon), WeLive, and Common Living, this industry has grabbed the attention of strategic investors and business tycoons who specialize in predicting future explosions in success. And this isn't just a personal theory. The Collective alone has received a cool $400 million in funding to expand. Common recently got over $63 million. The numbers here speak for themselves. Investors want in. Let's talk about why that is, exactly.

How it All Started

Coliving has existed in practice long before the term itself was coined. Even back in the 19th and 20th centuries, there are records of coliving homes designed as boarding spaces. But the concept was the same. I'm confident that they were around long before this point too, just not by name. These same models have existed across countless countries and social groups. A lot of the time, they were being created in different parts of the world without the knowledge that others were doing it too. Coincidence? We think not. People have instinctually gravitated to this system because it works. Regardless of the specific characteristics of these communities, coliving has provided the ability to unite individuals with one another and create an overall better quality of life across personal and professional boundaries. We're hoping to revive this concept and remind people that, although the idea isn't new, it fits our modern needs better than anything else.

As the third urban revolution incites global societal shifts in what it means to be connected, our world is responding by reimagining what a home now means. Modern definitions of transportation, shopping, and travel have all been subverted, and now is the time that the notion of housing enters a period of incredible revival as well. Recently, coworking has exploded as a welcomed disruption to the business environment which indicates that this movement toward shared spaces proves effective and is here to stay. However, although globalization has expanded the distance at which various work can be completed, it is becoming clear that communication can develop anywhere, but authentic relationships cannot. The importance of human interaction is something that adds unparalleled value to any line of work, as well as feeds our natural inclination to obtain rewarding connections. This is the value of coliving. People are realizing that proximity allows for interplay and success that virtual links cannot provide; there is an inherent value to human engagement that our digital society still demands. In response to this, the rise of coliving seeks to solve these problems with one cohesive solution. Its fusion of work, home, and play allows for individuals to nourish all parts of their life without compartmentalizing them into independent (and often incomplete) facets. People are beginning to discover that there are strategic solutions, or 'hacks', to solving current challenges that virtually everyone faces.

The rise of the coliving industry has also been catalyzed by shifts in how space is regarded. In past years across the globe, individuals are moving to big cities at unparalleled rates. This motivation to seek residence in urban areas stems from the recognition that surrounding oneself with fresh ideas, diversity, and innovation allows for optimal growth in all respects. However, as the populations of cities continue to rise, available space responds inversely. In order to accommodate these vast numbers, our theoretical construction of space has to change. Luckily, it is. Although individuals and families alike are increasingly opting for less room in exchange for a favorable location, this tradeoff comes with a hefty price tag. Coliving intercepts this issue by maintaining one's ability to situate themselves in a strategic geographic place, but also keep costs reasonable. At the same time, coliving offers valuable amenities which residents would likely not be able to obtain if seeking a place on their own. Even when located outside of cities, coliving retains these valuable attributes in the same sense. When a coliving space is created in remote locations, such as a tropical island, it offers the productive and interactive dynamic that cities provide while allowing members to also pursue the surroundings that they most desire.

Shifting demands for efficiency also underscore the rising appeal of coliving. Recognizing the worldwide increase in population which coincides with an unprecedented use of limited resources, our society faces the challenge of finding new ways to provide everyone with the basic necessities required. Modern solutions to overflowing cities, such as Smart Growth and New Urbanism approaches, have made valiant strides toward reconstructing residential layouts to suit our shifting demographics. From an environmental perspective, coliving also acts as a promising solution on the rise. This is because residents of a coliving home use far less space per person and operate from shared resources, thus reducing each individual footprint and also minimizing waste. However, it's natural that people still crave their personal alone time at certain points. Again, coliving has an answer to this. By designating areas in a home that are communal while keeping other spaces completely private, this arrangement offers the best of both worlds. Coliving allows for an ideal balance in which members feel no compromise between space, privacy, location, productivity, and fulfillment.

The coliving industry has garnered attention as a result of priority transformations. Specifically, the new generation of successful people in the workforce is also marked by an altered set of values. Currently, dwellers in the professional realm are making it clear that experiences and relationships are of utmost priority, not just income and wealth. It just so happens that coliving, while fostering a sense of community and satisfaction that is paramount to most, also simultaneously lifts the quality of work that these residents are able to do. For young individuals who are in the process of a more mobile lifestyle at the outset of their careers, coliving also provides the flexibility to move across different cities and locations as a young professional without feeling any compromise in feasibility or isolation.

In addition, the increased interest in coliving has stemmed from the desire for individuals to personally define and create the space they desire, as opposed to operating within a pre-established framework. By tailoring one's living space to their exact needs, residents regain control over this part of their lives. Having your own input on your space isn't a new concept, but it has gotten a bit lost over the last few decades as home builders decided what they thought we would like from a home. Identikit house building was an easy way for the few to make money from the masses. The trend of building your own space and making it personal to your life is growing again. The simple fact of the matter is that coliving is a natural extension of this.

In modern society, there remains a great deal of reliance on large corporations to produce what we need and to accept this without much question or choice. However, this appears to be a thing of the recent past. Millennials have changed the game. They don't accept the status quo. They challenge what is around and look for alternatives. If these alternatives don't exist yet on the open market, they produce the solution themselves.

Space. There's enough of it but we are still concerned about not having our fair share. That's where coliving comes in. This is where this idea takes shape more than ever.

Many coliving homes have also gained popularity due to their ability to provide dwellers with a greater sense of safety. The presence of more advanced security measures than they would be able to obtain independently includes cameras, secure entry, and a more extensive selection process for the other residents they will be surrounded with. In doing so, individuals have solid confidence in the wellbeing of themselves and their property. We can't underestimate safety as a vital component of the way we live. It underpins the way we do everything else. If we don't feel safe, then we don't really have the freedom, either physically or psychologically, to be ourselves. That can be a frightening place to be in this world.

Priorities have changed too. Some of them through necessity, others through the changing of society. The price of property is a major factor in this. It used to be one of the passages of life in many major economies to move from the parental home into a place of your own. But property is now seen as much as an investment or replacement for the pension as it is a place to live. This shift in attitude means that property prices have risen on the back of investment funds and speculators buying up property in the hope or expectation of a return. This has forced people to look differently at their ability to buy a property. It is simply more difficult to do than it was a generation ago. Added to this is the continuing reluctance of mortgage lenders to release cash in the same way they did in the past. The financial crisis of 2008 is still having a profound effect on the appetite for lenders to release money to mortgage borrowers in the same way they did before. There is a school of thought that they shouldn't lend in the same manner as before. This irresponsibility is, after all, what led us to the credit crunch. But they err on the side of caution. Younger people struggle to get a mortgage when they need one.

At the same time, society doesn't see property in the same way as it did. Millennials don't desire property, the home, or the same life trajectory that the baby boomer generation did, for instance. As this attitude becomes more widespread, you can see more millennial ideals coming together. Collaboration and spending time socializing are vitally important to the way millennials see their life. Coliving is the perfect way to ensure these ideals are catered to and people can feel comfortable in what they do.

For these reasons, coliving has emerged not as a last resort for struggling individuals, but for thriving visionaries who may easily have the means to acquire a large space of their own, but just consciously choose not to. With this in mind, coliving may very well be the perfect fit for you (as it is for millions of others). Read on to find out exactly how.

Two

My Story

It's funny. I have lived alone before, but actually prefer living with roommates.

Living with roommates first started as a necessity due to affordability and the fact that I had a dog for 11 years and needed the extra help since I worked crazy hours and traveled a bit. I always had wonderful roommates who loved having a dog around and would take good care of him.

So, my history with coliving goes back at least 13 years. I first did it in San Diego, California, in the Mission Valley area. I had a 3-bedroom townhome for 10 years there and loved it.

In the beginning, just by chance, I lived with two nurses that worked at a hospital. I found them separately through Craigslist and then they became friends. After that, I lived with military guys. I learned that, when I put up an ad, it helped to specify if there was a certain type of person I wanted to live with. Honestly, I've found the most amazing roommates through Craigslist. We actually still use that platform to this day to find housemates, but we'll get more into that later on.

I knew that nurses and military members were both typically very clean, organized, and dependable types of people and that's why I often tended to write that in the ad. Now, I realized that the reason they would usually become friends with one another is because they had a common interest (this time being their profession) and it just made for such a better living environment. Again, this all happened before coliving was even a word. There was more harmony in the home when we had like-minded people living together.

And I've lived with different people too. I've ran the gamut in the last 13 years. It was so cool to live alongside people who came from different parts of the world, different religions, upbringings, etc. I learned so much and it also really opened my eyes to certain preconceived notions that I was exposed to due to being brought up in a more limited environment as a child.

In the last two years, I have lived solely with entrepreneurs. Again, it's nice to be around like-minded people who get me, work hard and sometimes crazy hours, are making their own rules and creating their own schedule versus living with people who have nine-to-five jobs. From experience, I know it is best when you live with people who are similar to you. A lot of people I've previously lived with, who have the typical nine-to-five jobs, would come home complaining about their boss or how much they hated Mondays and loved Fridays. But in an entrepreneur's life, we're incredibly excited for Mondays and genuinely pumped to get things going. The amazing power of this energy has such an impact on our happiness and how we grind to get work done. Energy is contagious!

Plus, living in cities like San Diego and Los Angeles is painfully pricey! When you live alone, you pay for all the utilities yourself, plus house cleaning, food, and rent. This alternative was just a better way for me to share my resources. Now I don't feel like I'm wasting things, especially as much as I travel, by living with multiple people in a large, beautiful home.

It was two or three years ago when I started really thinking, 'how cool it would be to have a house of just entrepreneurs living together.' Fast forward a year or two later, I'm telling my mentor this idea; but I still owned my spa at the time, so I was way too busy to flesh out the concept.

Once I finally got into a space that I was sharing with fellow entrepreneurs, my network in business exploded. My business even grew just from being in there for those few weeks because I was around all my typical clients, the people that I wanted to help, which are entrepreneurs. I met the most amazing people. I met so many people that our networks quadrupled, because you have your own network, and then you have the networks of your four roommates that they're bringing into the house on a regular basis. So I lived with them for a year and a half while I was still building out my spa. The spa sold in November of 2017. And at that point, I realized I had this full-fledged idea that I couldn't ignore; I just had to dive in. So I started Kindred Quarters. I'm still super close to those roommates; they're like brothers to me. And we still hang out at one of the houses or go to dinner together. I'm so grateful that we've all remained so connected.

And that's how Kindred Quarters was born. Next, we opened a house in Mission Hills, and then a second house in Mission Hills, which is where economies of scale kick in. Since we have the same chef for both houses, they come in daily and do food prep for both properties every single day. We also have a concierge that goes between the two homes. We learned how much that drove all the costs down across the board. When someone is shopping once for both houses and cooking all the meals at once for both houses, it makes a huge difference. And it had the capacity to do three easily, plus we had lots of friends wanting to move in; so we opened up a third one in the same neighborhood soon after.

We call it lifestyle design. It's kind of our joke. We literally have everything outsourced, like cleaning our cars, dry cleaning, and even little things like cutting lemons so that we can just grab them out of a container and throw them in our water each morning. It sounds kind of silly at first, but we've realized that every little thing you can minimize the time on is going to help you grow your company even faster. This is because you don't have to think of all these little things, it's just done for you. That's really what we wanted to build. We wanted to first outsource as much as we could, and also build community. Which ended up happening amazingly fast because we have tons of events, which allowed us to not only build community with each other, but also expand these circles. We network with each other, but we also throw events and bring outside people in to build that community. It's honestly so much fun.

This is question I get asked the most: But how do you get any privacy? Well, I still have my own private bedroom to retreat to for some downtime by myself. I don't feel like I have to be around my fellow housemates all of the time. Plus, most of them travel and work a ton too so there have been numerous times where I have a huge 6-bedroom property all to myself.

I am obviously a huge advocate for coliving and really excited to see the $200 trillion real estate industry get flipped around and revived, just like Uber did with transportation and Airbnb to the hotel industry.

For people to qualify for a space in the first house, we had income requirements and actual gross revenue requirements. Your company had to be doing at least six figures a year, so $100,000 or more in gross revenue. They were really strict about that. However, there were people that I feel like had so much potential that would have contributed a lot to the house but they were just starting out. So for the second house, nicknamed the "Entourage House," it was a seven figure minimum. Everybody in the house was doing seven figures or more a year. Although this was how it started out, I really feel like you can learn so much from somebody even making a lot less than you. I can remember a roommate in one of our other homes that was making a lot, lot less, but I learned more from him than anybody. In the next house we were a lot more open. The only income requirement was that I wanted to know their net income just to be sure that they'd have enough money to pay rent, obviously. But we relaxed some of those monetary stipulations because I don't think it's as important as I thought it was before. What really matters is that it's somebody who is positive, driven, not lazy, who is contributing to the world in some way or another, and is just a cool person and somebody you like being around. I think that's more important to us than just how much your company is generating in revenue.

The really cool part of Kindred Quarters and this concept overall is that you can actually switch across one house to another very easily. For example, we're going international this year and are looking at either Bangkok or Chiang Mai, Thailand. That's probably going to be the next one, because we have people out there. The next place is Dubai, which is a place that a lot of us love. We're building an App out to connect all these homes really easily. I'll be able to jump on the Kindred Quarters App and say that I want to head to Australia for the month, then see if anybody wants to trade me for San Diego. So they'd come to stay in my room for a month, and I'd go to Australia for a month, so we're literally just doing a straight trade. This consistency means it's the same system: you walk into this place in a country you've never been, but you know that your food is going to be on your shelf as requested, you know there's Bulletproof coffee every morning available, and there's a sense of familiarity. All the systems and structure are already there, so you almost feel like it's home, even in a brand new country. You can travel somewhere or go to some new location, but at the same time keep that consistent environment of people that are supporting you and helping you grow your business.

We're getting all those different aspects that you enjoy with being in Kindred Quarters, but you're also traveling and seeing the world while going to these different new locations. Plus, you can meet new people, expand your network internationally, and hang out with them for the month. They're sure to show you around the country. This is the part I'm super excited about. I'm finally able to find a way to mix the three things I'm the most passionate about: real estate, business, and travel. I realized this was the way to do it. And I'm excited for you to join the tribe!

Three

Tribe

You have probably already heard the quote by Jim Rohn, "**You are the average of the five people you spend the most time with.**"

Why is it important to live with other people? And why live with similar people? We are all brought up in one way or another. The family unit is still seen as a strong way to bring up children and to live. But we move away from the family home into other things before starting a family of our own in many instances. We can move somewhere because of work, to be close to someone else, or because it's our dream city to live in. But not all of these reasons mean we wind up living in a place with others, or with others that we are similar to. Similarity is an often an overlooked value. We take it for granted that the person or people we live with are the same or similar to us because of geographical reasons or that we will learn to like each other over time. Sharing a place with other human beings can feel quite daunting to some.

The importance of social interaction is highlighted in the mental health issues we are facing as a nation and across the globe. People are becoming more isolated and more depressed, even as technology expands its ability to bring us closer together. We often speak to people via Text Message or Facebook Messenger rather than in person, even if that person lives close by. It does little for social and emotional health. The solution is to live among others. However, in order to be beneficial, this solution also needs to take into account that some others might not be the ideal candidates to help us on our life journey. So we look for similar people to have this meaningful life or lifestyle experience with. But they are not always easy to find. This is why coliving is such a fulfilling experience. We can live with others that share a passion for the things in life that are important to us- without the downsides.

You should look for others that feel strongly about the things you feel strongly about. From the very start of the process of considering coliving, you should have a clear idea of what is important to you. Once you get a solid grasp of what this is, then you know what you are looking for. Far too often we put the cart before the horse. We look for a place near to work or a place in a certain budget. Sure, these are certainly important factors in selecting a place to live, but it is far more essential to find people that will help us on the journey. Think about the inspiration you have for life. If there are others around that can feed your imagination and help you to visualize the positive future you are headed for, then it is far more likely to become a reality. Surrounding yourself with people who think and act like you is a lifestyle choice that will help you to explore who you are and become a better person. This truth is undeniable.

Openness and honesty are the cornerstones of a successful living arrangement, whether that is part of a family, shared accommodation, or coliving. If you have these as part of your daily life, then all manner of good things happen as a result. We will see throughout the course of this book that there are a number of legal steps you should also take to cover yourself and anyone else you live with for that matter. But they are just the backup. The real joy comes from finding people that you truly want to share this leg of your race with. The beauty is living with people who make you feel alive.

So, let's look at how all of this works. This book is designed to help you figure out what coliving looks like for you. There is an infinite number of coliving variations, so we won't be looking at a step-by-step set of instructions that lead you from today to a coliving future. You will be able to make this exactly as you want it (form it in your own image if you like) so that the coliving experience delivers just what you want it to. Make notes as you go. They will help you work out what it is you want and how to get out there and make it happen.

The Importance of Living with Like-Minded People

It is no secret that shared visions align together well. When someone is searching for an employee or business partner, these ideological and experiential attributes are often painstakingly analyzed to ensure a good fit. However, this notion is not always adhered to as closely when it comes to finding a housemate. This is really a glaring misstep, as the quality of one's surroundings are massively integral to the ability to work effectively and be fulfilled. Energy is not just a thing of philosophy; it's always around and can be felt in shockingly tangible ways when you take a look at performance and results. With the right atmosphere, unbelievable strides can be made. With the wrong one, however, progress can grind to a standstill or even regress. In truth, we humans are social beings. We yearn to be accepted by those who are able to adopt a similar perspective. Coliving allows for just that- an environment in which alike individuals can be validated and understood by others around them, fostering a positive kinship. For those who are fiercely committed to their pursuits and projects, it can be really lonely and incur a sense of isolation. The frustration and obstacles that come with innovation are uniquely arduous, as any of you entrepreneurs out there must know. But sharing this experience with others in the same position is often all a person needs to reinvigorate their motivation to persevere. At the same time, these surrounding members can also challenge one another and force them to think differently, broadening their mental horizons to a point of unparalleled growth. No matter how much you already know, there's always more to learn.

This does not mean that coliving is (or should be) an echo chamber. While it's true that coliving is instinctually based upon similarities, it simultaneously offers members an opportunity to experience diversity in other ways. Although fundamental lifestyle and professional tenets may be the same, coliving allows residents to engage with housemates of other ages or stages of life, business trajectories, different cultural and social backgrounds, and all parts of the world. These unique variations provide the enriching experience of enhanced knowledge, acceptance, and global networks. Coliving gives members the personal advantage to come into contact with new valuable connections that their housemates can introduce them to. This ability to form partnering relationships for the present and future broadens each individual's social circle, situating them advantageously for business pursuits as well as outside advice and input.

With this in mind, there's no reason to settle for an environment that is anything but positive and encouraging. It's entirely possible, too. All you need to do is align yourself with the right people who create a collective energy that coincides with your own. A coliving space is the perfect way to achieve this. In order to do so, it's essential to follow a series of personal steps in order to be positioned properly for this opportunity. First, you can start with a list. Write down each of the morals, basic values, rules of integrity, and basic mindset that you find most intrinsic. This can apply to yourself as well as those which you seek in a housemate (although they may often be the same). In doing so, it is important to also detail the intricate components of daily living, such as cleanliness, ideal degree of interaction, and lifestyle habits. It may also be valuable to include things that you know are definite deal-breakers, perhaps from past experience. These recognized dislikes are equally helpful in order to rule out things at the beginning that you know will not be viable, which will save you time and money by preventing you from entering into an agreement that may end badly (or costly).

Honesty is the golden policy in this process. For example, although you may like to believe that you are an extremely neat person and seek housemates who operate the same, this is not productive if you simply want others to be tidy but do not do so in your own life. In other words, do not kid yourself. When you come into contact with a prospective match, be sure to allocate ample time to engage with them in-person. It is not ideal to base your final decision off a single brief meeting. Be sure to get to know them on a more personal level; living with someone is an intimate thing and it takes longer to truly know someone than the brief duration it takes to grab a coffee. As challenging as it may be for some people, honesty is imperative. Don't approach a potential housemate from the lens of seeking to impress them. Instead, try to portray yourself in the most authentic manner that they would actually be seeing you in the living space.

Coliving is built upon a foundation of synergy between all members of the tribe. For this reason, the process of securing a spot within these coveted spaces should be anything but easy. A detailed entry process ensures that any new member in question is not only being placed into the ideal home for their lifestyle, but that those in the space are also equally benefiting from it too. As a whole, the relationship between all members of a coliving tribe should be mutualistic. This means that a fairly extensive series of steps is necessary to ensure the right fit.

The first point of access in this process is a simple questionnaire. This provides an initial look into the basic goals, lifestyle, and expectations that a prospective member holds. After completing this, the personal interaction comes into play. Applicants who appear to share key qualities for a successful coliving home will probably undergo a quick phone conversation in order to gauge the personality of an individual, which cannot always be captured on paper.

There are some really solid reasons behind surrounding yourself with people that share the same values and think the way you do. Some of these are underappreciated in life. Think about how easy you find it to be yourself. If this is a challenge, then it may be because you are with people who don't think like you. The ability to be yourself is a safe and comforting place to be in life. It means you can talk openly and honestly about your hopes and fears, the way you see your life, and all the unanswered questions you may have. This can only truly happen if you are in that safe and trusting place to be vulnerable. You will find that you flourish and develop as a person when you are at in this place in your life. You get inspired and motivated to do things with your life that you likely didn't before.

But there are also consequences to NOT surrounding yourself with like-minded individuals. This can be a more of a motive to some than the positives. The downsides scare some away from a path as much as the upsides keep others moving towards a goal. With this in mind, you can vary your marketing to appeal to both these types of people. They can be defined as people who go towards something or people that move away from something.

You can feel alienated if you don't have this connection to like-minded people in your life. This means you might end up thinking that all relationships are like this. You could start to think that you can't be a good friend or work colleague because you have never experienced fantastic relationships like the ones you're aiming to grow with a coliving space. This can have a hugely detrimental effect on your emotional wellness. You lose connection to your hopes and dreams. You stop aiming high.

Being part of a tribe is now seen as an excellent way to live. Great businesses use the tribe concept to look after the team of people they employ for maximum results. The feeling of belonging that comes from being part of a tribe is amazing. It gets the people in that business to work together for the common goal. It pulls communities of people to the same cause. In the case of the coliving collective, the tribe is a group of people that all feel the same way about life. This can come from experience, background, or work. It can, in fact, stem from a number of different things. There is an air of the intangibility about the tribe. The truest tribes cannot always put their finger on why they stay together and belong. But they know they do.

The concept itself harks back to Native Americans and the ways in which they all worked together for the common good. They looked out for each other and fulfilled roles that allowed the tribe to prosper. Even today, when a tribe member is struggling, they focus on restoring the individual and family, rather than casting them out or punishing, as our state penal system opts for. In your coliving potential, your tribe doesn't have the same exact challenges such the hunt for food and constant need to battle the elements, but you do have the collective urge to pull together and make this a better life. Working together in a group space where all feel happy, comfortable, and accepted is the ideal way to build something that is much greater than the sum of its parts.

Exclusive or NOT Exclusive?

It's not always easy to find enough people who perfectly fit into a finite group, especially at the outset of forming a coliving home. Although you may have a vision of how specific you want the space to be in terms of who is admitted, this may not be quite so feasible when starting out. Or, it's possible that you want to make the space open to a broad variety of potential housemates, without imposing as many limitations. However, this does not mean compromising key values for the home. There are some great reasons to be as selective as possible. You can work with the ethics of the group and build a small community of people that synergize and work together to become something more than a collective of people. But it will almost inevitably take more time to find those people. There is a value in it, but the time factor comes into play. Nothing great is easy. On the other hand, you could look at getting people in as quickly as possible in order to get on with your dream, but they may not all fit into the philosophy as neatly as you had imagined at the outset.

Exclusivity is something that can help you recruit in the long run when your coliving business is fully formed and there are rivals on the market competing with you for potential housemates. This is the time that you can decide to put things in place for that eventuality. You can always consult a legal expert on fair housing and equal rights to make sure these are being adhered to as well, of course! Thinking about making your property exclusive now will set you up for later. You can differentiate in the market on more than one thing. Many think that the best way to distinguish what they offer is by price. You'll see low prices, promotions, and offers in retailers all over the world, all trying to compete for the precious attention of their target market. But there are also successful retailers that don't compete on price. Their fees are higher because they provide better quality products and services. These companies still thrive because they are offering the consumer a choice. They can afford to spend more time with each client due to the higher margins created by their steeper prices.

Likewise, you can offer a better service and a better quality living space if you charge a higher price per person. You should do some research to confirm that your target market will sustain this, but in essence, you can make the property exclusive and reap the rewards from this if you have the right marketing and business plan to back it up. There are lots of ways that you can make sure this happens. Just look at the sections in this book and think about the different levels of service and the ranging price points that go with them. For example, when you think of hiring a chef, there is a difference between a Michelin-star rated chef and one that has worked in kitchens for a year or two. When you decorate a property, there is also a vast difference in the quality of decoration and furniture- think Ikea versus high end and you'll know what I mean. Same goes with tech amenities.

Think about the communities that you already belong to. You may find that there are people currently in your network that are perfectly fitted to the coliving experience you are looking to develop. Approach them! You might not find that they are looking for a new space at this moment in time, but they'll still be able to help you potentially find others and develop your ideals on what your coliving space would look like. The more information (basically market research) that you have, the better you can refine your research and make everything you do look and feel more realistic.

Marketing Sources (Word of Mouth)

Although the perfect housemates are out there, the ability to find one another is a whole new challenge. Make use of the vast array of marketing options that can be used to get the word out about your coliving home in an authentic way. However, don't discount word of mouth as a valuable player in this dimension. When it comes to seeking out the perfect partners to fit into a lifestyle, starting with personal connections is a great place to begin because it is built upon a foundation of genuine personal knowledge of one another. Word of mouth also generates an organic buzz around the space, creating productive conversations in the right circles to reach your target groups of similar values. Imagine the conversations happening in workplaces, gyms, and other hangouts when talking about your coliving space. If you have an exciting space or idea then it will create exciting conversations. People will want to live with you and want to be a part of the group. That makes recruiting new housemates a whole lot easier. If you don't have to persuade people, you can also save money on advertising.

Word of mouth only goes so far, though. Although it is by far the most effective, quickest, and most reliable way to find people for your coliving space, there may be times when you have to bite the bullet and advertise (especially at the beginning when things are new). This might be an expense that you wish to avoid, but it can also be worth it. The next best thing to effective word of mouth advertising is effective social media advertising, so take a look at how you can make this happen. Social media is a tool that, when used well, can help you get the right exposure for your coliving space without cost and can also generate a true following.

You may draw a blank with these two areas and think that you need to spend money on advertising. If this is the case, then you need to look at your paid advertising with these two things at the forefront of your mind:

1. Who is my target market?
2. Where do they hang out?

These are vital questions that will determine the results you gain from any paid marketing campaign. You should look at this like you would the spend with a business. Return On Investment is a massive term in the business world, and this is no different when you are looking to find people for your coliving space. Basically, you don't want to spend a thousand dollars attracting a housemate that will bring in five hundred bucks in income. Or even worse, spending a grand to find nobody at all. Instead, look at where your target audience spends their time. If this is predominantly online, then offline advertising won't exactly bring in the response you require. If this is in the center of a city, then advertising in the suburbs doesn't help you either. This is the basic research you will need to do well in advance to get yourself on the right track. If you have a vacancy in your coliving home, then this unfilled space is costing you money every day. Getting the right advertising in the right space puts the cash back into your pocket and keeps things moving along progressively.

In here, we'll also cover press releases, blogging, and all that fun stuff. These are incredibly helpful for keeping the excitement going when you are trying to recruit your tribe, build your community, and get the right exposure. Consider using Medium as an amazing free resource to either have your own blog platform or just follow others. You can check out current accounts like Kindred Quarters and your favorite inspirational people to get ideas for articles to post yourself or just to read and keep aware of what's new. Medium also allows you to search by topic and keywords to hone pieces within your areas of interest and connect with others who enjoy the same ideas.

The next step is writing a press release. We've already had a couple published for Kindred Quarters. Overall, this is how you guys are going to push out information and distribute it, which is KEY to visibility. In terms of frequency, realistically, once a quarter is a good gauge to do these. It's a reasonable timeline to actually write the press release and make sure that the quality is there. It's got to be good, especially to get picked up!

In the entrepreneur houses, there has been tons of success with getting articles out and into the right eyes. The first is Eric Yang, who lived at the Epic Entrepreneur House a couple years ago. He got an amazing piece submitted, and Influencive.com is a great site to get published on. Another example is Chandler Bolt, who actually created the Epic Entrepreneur House three years ago. His got picked up by Entrepreneur Magazine online in August of 2016.

The bottom line here is that you really have to try, submit, and push repeatedly to get into these larger publications online. But it's completely doable. And when it does happen, you can put them on your website, share them on your social media, and generally make it known that you guys got picked up, which equals awesome press for your coliving house. This not only makes yours easier to find but also speaks to its notability and quality.

There's also lots that can be done on YouTube. An easy start is to do some interviews and put them on up your channel. It helps to explain your entire concept as well as drive more traffic by linking to all your social media below on every single YouTube video posted. The more platforms driving visibility plus conversion and getting your stuff out there, the better!

Video content doesn't have to stop at interviews—feel free to get creative. If you need some inspiration, go to other YouTube channels for ideas. We like to offer different types of content including testimonials of our residents and walkthroughs of the homes to get a feel for the dynamic of the spaces and generate excitement about what life there is like. It's also fun to do videos of our parties and events by making little trailers to get people looking forward to the next one. This can take a bit of time when all is considered with the filming and editing, so try to block off a day or so every couple weeks to really dive in.

Three Personal References
It's important to take into account the testimonies of others to reinforce the quality of your potential housemates. By asking for these references, reputable individuals can attest to the character composition of applicants in an authentic way. These can also be used to understand your possible members in various lights by getting outside opinions on their social and professional history. The potential issues that can arise from sharing a living space with others can be frightening if you directly follow them to their end conclusion

at times. But there's no need to be scared of what might happen if you get proper and thorough referencing. It's not hard to do!

Coliving is a safe way to live. Getting referencing right means you can relax with new members of the space because you know a lot of their background already. If you get references that cause any concern, then it's probably best to err on the side of caution. Any doubt means you should probably consider looking elsewhere. Don't be afraid to trust your gut either!

That's the way it is when looking at people to occupy a living space with you. There can't be any element of doubt involved. Settling for the next best fit can lead to problems in the whole collective. If one person comes in and is disruptive, then the whole ecosystem can fall apart pretty quickly and in spectacular fashion. You could wind up losing the good people you have and might have to start all over again. Going back to the drawing board at the interview process is better than accepting someone who doesn't fit the delicate jigsaw you've been painstakingly putting together.

Video Application
A valuable and modern approach to securing your ideal tribe is by including a video application element. This provides some insight into how housemates approach projects and their abilities across different creative and analytical skill sets. Some inventive coliving practitioners will use Skype or even Snapchat to 'interview' potential applicants and build a kind of relationship with them before offering the space on an ongoing basis. Think about the best methods for your group to meet and build connections with people before you commit. Look at it in a similar way as online dating. You'd check out the profile and maybe message casually at first. When you have a better idea of what the person is like, then you might arrange to meet them in a public place. After that you can start to think about more meetings and

something a little longer term if it goes well. The same applies to finding coliving partners. You'll want to find out more about the compatibility when you make contact and maintain this for a short period of time during the selection process.

Lease Paperwork

To ensure that you're legally covered when creating a coliving space, you should set up all the necessary documents that offer protection for all of the people concerned. If you are leasing out certain parts of the space rather than buying as a group, then you should always get lease documents drawn up by a legal professional. Don't leave any room for doubt or interpretation when living together. Unfortunately, there may be the odd occasion where a small dispute occurs. It can often be about something simple and easy to resolve. If you have legal documentation signed by all parties, then you always have that fallback reference to point to and the issue stops there. The best way to resolve any situation like this is through dialog and positivity, but when push comes to shove, you want to be able to exercise your rights through the legal process. Getting people to sign on the dotted line gives you a much stronger and healthier legal position should this rare occurrence ever actually arise.

It can be really tempting to rely on trust. After all, if that isn't one of the major things you are creating with your coliving space, then what else is this about? While this is true, trust can only take you so far. It's still comforting to have this reinforcement in your arsenal regardless of how well you all get along. Lease agreements look after both parties. I like to look at it as trust with a backup. We all trust each other enough to sign a lease agreement that gives both sides rights and responsibilities, right? With people who are all on the same page, this shouldn't be a problem.

Housemate Retention

You should think long and hard about finding the right housemates. It's important to keep a close eye on the retention component of your home because that's how you are able to build deep connections and bonds that make coliving so valuable. The first step to keeping quality coliving people is (of course) to select the right housemates in the first place. Look again through all of the information above to ensure you have a robust selection process that winds up with you finding the right people. This puts you in the best position to keep your quality housemates.

Retention of residents is important. It helps to build the feel you want for your space. Otherwise, it will take time to embed new people into the way you operate and make them feel at home at the same time. The longer people stay, the better it looks when you do have a vacancy and are looking to recruit. You should keep figure on retention if this is your business as you can start to see the metrics unfold over time. If people stay in your coliving space for an average of 3 years, for example, then this will help you to market to relevant people when you need a space filled. If the people you speak to want something shorter term than that, then they may not be the ideal fit you are looking for. All of this data you can keep on your business will help you to understand it better and improve or refine what you offer in the future.

You want to make sure to deliver all you promised. If you advertised a living space as calm and peaceful, then you should provide that environment for those people or they won't stay for very long. There will be an expense to find new people, whether it's an investment of time or money. A period of disruption can often occur when a house member moves out and another enters. Whatever the reason is for changing housemates, there will probably be a physical and emotional upheaval at this point in time. Doing your best to minimize the number of times you have a new housemate situation will help everyone involved. A feeling of stability is a much happier place to live than one where housemates are circulating on a regular basis.

It's ideal having some core people in the home. Again, it's your house so you can choose to operate however you want, but a core group is highly recommended. Maybe it's four of you in a five bedroom, with the fifth bedroom on weekly or monthly rotations. This injects some fresh new energy in there and allows you to meet new people. We've done variations of this in most past homes and it's a component that people really love. Shorter rotations for some rooms provide just enough time to build those connections and then have somebody new.

However, keeping this core group together is huge. You're bound to get to know each other on an intimate level and have amazing conversations which is incredibly important on the retention side. A lot of times it's not about the house, the area, the food—none of that really matters as much as those connections you have with the people in these homes. The people who have lived in these spaces often remain close friends and confidants even long after moving out.

Definitely do monthly check-ins. Don't assume that there's harmony in the house for everyone, even if it may seem to be the case. Sit down with each person and take 30 minutes to discuss what's going right in the home and what can be improved on. Even if you host weekly Masterminds and talk about house items then, it's valuable to designate a separate time aside once a month to find out how each person is feeling. Be constantly evolving, and constantly improving the environment you guys are creating.

For obtaining more short-term residents, Airbnb is also an element to use when looking to make the most of the space you have. Make sure to create the right listing that attracts your ideal people and figure out what to charge realistically. Ask yourself a variety of questions. What kind of people do you want to bring in? Do you want to open it up to anybody? Do you want to limit it strictly to entrepreneurs? Both have been done before and have their benefits.

Craigslist, believe it or not, is still an amazing way to find qualified housemates. Again, you just need be sure to write the correct ad to attract the right person. Lastly, constantly recruit. One of the biggest ways to recruit is not only word of mouth, but also by hosting events. If there's a time you're really pressed to find somebody to take a room, then host an amazing event to fill it up ASAP. One idea that's had success is a vision board party, where you can invite a bunch of people with some great food to recruit others, because people can see and experience the environment. Even if you aren't scrambling to fill a spot, it can be fun to launch Sunday night barbecues to invite outside guests with an open house style.

Four

Community

List of Values
Don't just assume that everyone else shares your same exact values-make them unquestionably clear. By creating a written list of the core tenets you find most important (both about living spaces and otherwise), you can best communicate these to prospective members. In doing so, this process also establishes your home in the social sphere for others who may be interested in finding you and makes it easy to distinguish if a prospective member fits in. Make sure these values span across all different areas, from personal outlook to codes of conduct which will apply to relevant situations in the house. These values dictate how issues are handled and also enable you to refer back to them and reflect on how your home is doing in terms of upholding them. Values are what are most important in all of this. You want to be able to go home to a relaxed and supportive environment. This reduces stress and allows us all to live the best life we can. If you arrive back to a home where you value peace and tranquility, but instead there's noise and partying until the small hours of the morning, it won't take long for things to become unpleasant. If it helps, write down all of the values that are vitally important to you and your life. From there, you'll be able to develop a structure with your fellow coliving members that works well for all.

Your values are what define you, but they are also what link people together. Major corporations work long and hard on their values and recruit people who fit into these rather than sourcing the right skills and hoping they fit into the values. Skills can be taught, but values aren't so easy. Think about what might be easier to develop: a set of functional skills or changing a behavior that has been prevalent throughout a person's life. I think if you look at things in this way, the answer is pretty easy to come by.

Mindset
This is a very important topic in the book. The value of mindset and personal goal setting is huge, and this is for you personally as the owner and the LEADER of your coliving home. You want to make sure that you start with your own mindset and your own goals before you start coaching and leading the other residents and guests in your homes on their own goals and mindset. Let's launch right into it.

Now, what I've been doing for years is, during my lunch break or any break, I actually log right into YouTube and just search for things. It just depends on what I'm working on at the time, but obviously YouTube has a wealth of knowledge and it's so easy to just turn on any video. Of course, some of my few favorites are Gary Vaynerchuk, Grant Cardone, or you could just type in an actual topic. You could put in "MOTIVATION," or you can type in an actual person that you enjoy following. Again, the more knowledge you gain makes it just that much easier to lead your home. Being able to **obtain** and **retain** knowledge is a literal gamechanger.

"Deciding what you want, believe that you can have it, believe you deserve it, and believe it's possible for you." This is an amazing quote, and it is so very true. I've included a couple of fun goal-setting exercises in this book that will show you exactly how to do it, and I promise it works like magic!

Now let's talk about the different personal development organizations out there. I can't vouch for all of these, but I have done some of them. I'm a huge fan of Toastmasters, I was a member for three years. 'EO', which is the Entrepreneurs Organization, is another amazing group. I have a lot of friends in it. I'm also a big fan of any masterminds. I've been in masterminds for at least 12 years, over a decade. Again, you're just getting outside perspective from people who know a ton, and that definitely helps because a lot of times you can get tunnel vision in your own life and business. A fresh, intelligent outlook is amazing.

Junto is a great organization. I'm currently a member of that group in San Diego. Another leadership and personal development group is the Landmark Forum, which I did about 12 years ago and then there is BNI (Business Networking International). I was in that for three years. Again, personal development organizations are an amazing way to grow your network and make those business connections.

Now remember, the stronger you become as a leader, the more successful you're going to be overall. Not just in running your home, but in business, in relationships, in friendships, in life, so it's always really important to make sure that personal development is high on your list of objectives.

Additionally, reading books to gain knowledge is another important thing to do. Actually, I have a new HACK for this. I've been an avid book reader forever and I have a huge physical book collection, but then I went to audiobooks and podcasts. So my physical book reading has decreased in the past couple years. However, a good friend of mine recently referred me over to Blinkist, which is an App on the phone that actually gives you the 'CliffsNotes' summaries of the best books, and now I'm flying through books again. It's just a 15-20 minute summary and it is both audio and visual, so you can **read along** and you can also **listen to it**, which, if you did not know this fun fact: If you use two senses (auditory AND visual) when taking in information, then you can actually retain more. Now, the best part is that if you like the summary of the book, then you can go buy the book. This is my number one hack for 2018. I'm such a Blinkist fan.

As for more mindset and goal-achieving hacks, here's another one for you. I don't know what's on your wallpaper of your phone, but I highly suggest making it something more goal-oriented, like a reward if you hit a certain goal, whether it's in your business or with your home that you're going to build. This is funny. I did this a year and a half ago with my dream car because I thought, "Well, gosh, I look at my phone so many times a day. What if I had it on there? Would that motivate me, maybe even subconsciously, to get this car?" Fast forward to now, I'm the very proud owner of a pretty sweet ride and I feel like that action is partly to thank for it.

Also be very mindful of the icons on your cell phone. This is another hack. I hide all the social media apps in a folder and I turn OFF all the notifications. However, on my main screen, I have an exercise APP, TRELLO for business management, my audiobook APP, and then the podcast APP. Then I have Spotify because I'm obsessed with listening to music all the time. Now, these are not social media apps. These are not time waster apps. These are making you a better person...Your career, your health, and growing your knowledge.

So please place the social media, the games, and any other non-value-adding apps over into a folder away from everything. The less distractions, the better. Then definitely turn off notifications, those little red notifications whenever you have a new message. I don't have any of those on my phone.

Here is a quick SUCCESS EXERCISE for this book, so go ahead and change the background of your phone. {I'll wait!} It could even be a motivational quote. That's even fine. It can be a heart if you're trying to find love. If you are getting ready to launch your own coliving home, maybe it is a picture of your dream house? Maybe the next house that you've got your eye on and are trying to get. For a little while there, we had an offer on a huge, beautiful home in San Diego for Kindred Quarters, so I had that house as my background for a couple of months. Unfortunately, the owner turned down the $2 million offer to purchase the home; it was no big deal—it just means it wasn't meant to be.

So start moving around your different apps on the phone, cleaning it up, and then picking what you want your image to be that ties to a big goal for your phone wallpaper. It doesn't need to be materialistic.

This is the Law of Attraction at work, whether or not you believe in it. From personal experience, I can tell you that it works. I watched The Secret back when it first came out like 10 years ago. I thought, "Okay, this is quite interesting." If you guys can run your house this way and teach others in your home these same tricks and tips and hacks, whatever you want to call them, it'll make your house that much more successful.

Next interactive SUCCESS EXERCISE:
"Shower goals."
Which you can download the template for free at:
ColivingCode.com/shower-goals

Okay. This is fun. What you do is you type out your goals for that current month. Then you print it up and put it in a laminated plastic protector sheet, so it does not get wet, then you tape it inside of your shower each month. You want to put the month and year at the top of the sheet. Then, you want to put your number one thing. Okay, guys. Do not get overwhelmed. Do not try to do everything. Please just focus on one thing. There's a great book called, "The One Thing." You guys should read it if you haven't, and just stay focused. That is the number one thing I see people, and especially entrepreneurs, doing wrong, is that they're not focused. They're all over the place and they overwhelm themselves by placing too many goals on themselves. I've been guilty of the same.

At the top, put your #1 focus for the month. Next, put your daily success habits, whether that's watching motivational videos on your lunch break, listening to one Blinkist book per day. Just something you will do every single day. Will you be at your desk at a certain time every morning? Or will you work out every day for 30 minutes? Do you have a specific nutrition plan for the month? In the next section on this same page, put your annual goals.

Okay, so I have five annual goals every year. I write those. You need to put them in your face every single day. If you write them on January 1st, never look at them again, then wonder why they didn't work at the end of the year, that does not work at all.

<<MONTH/YEAR>> :

<<YOUR ONE THING!>>

REVENUE GENERATING FOCUS:

~
~
~

DAILY SUCCESS HABITS:

**
**
**

You can create ANY LIFE that you want to create for yourself!

ANNUAL GOALS

~
~
~
~
~

It's all a game. | I love it. | I LIVE for this stuff. | Let's Do This!!!!

What are you GRATEFUL for TODAY?

Download the template for free at:
colivingcode.com/shower-goals

Then the last part is, "What are you grateful for today?" With a lot of success, the root of it comes from gratitude, so just make sure you guys are practicing that daily. Again, you're in the shower hopefully every day, so you'll see this every day, right? It's the one thing that I thought, "What the heck do I do every single day where I have this in my face?" I've tried putting it on my nightstand and looking at it before bed. That's still a struggle. Yeah. If you guys can look at it twice a day, that's even better. I've been trying to do that for the life of me, and it hasn't worked. Actually, I have a friend that does $200 million a year in annual revenue. He looks at it first thing in the morning, and the last thing at night, because when you're sleeping, a lot of times your subconscious can work on these things, so put an extra copy on your nightstand.

I actually have a video on Vimeo talking about Shower Goals. You could search my name on Vimeo to find it; I'll never take it down. It's from six years ago and it's hilarious because I filmed it right out of the shower, still in a towel.

I would love for you to set a great example as a contributor in your home, even if you are not the actual leader of the home. I learned so much from the leader of the first Epic Entrepreneur house I lived in from 2015–2017, Chandler Perog. He really paved the way for success for every individual in that home. You want to do the same if you decide you want to lead your own home. If you are sleeping in, not working, eating crappy, not exercising, that's not probably not going to work.

Everyone wants to be in an environment and in a home with people that are inspiring, that they look up to, and that they can learn from, grow with, have fun with, and build relationships with.

If you do decide to be the leader of your home, be sure to confidently grab the reins and be that that resource that they can come to you for support. It was nice for me to kind of pull back for that year in a half in that first home and not be a leader, and just concentrate on my last company, Eco Chateau Wellness Spa.

Please take the time now to print and fill out your shower goals; that will be your homework after this chapter. Also, make sure you already updated your smartphone by changing your wallpaper to something inspiring and motivating.

Since coliving is based on a reframed notion of community living, a shared quality of this lifestyle is that the tribe must occupy a similar mindset. This includes core outlooks on life, happiness, and success, as well as how coliving factors into these aspects. It's a blast when all Housemates encompass synonymous goals and values, which are key to building one another up. It is common knowledge that we as humans are strongly influenced by those surrounding us, whether we

44

like it or not. For this reason, fundamentals should be the same. Successful coliving experiences can exist between many different communities of interest, such as driven entrepreneurs, health enthusiasts, artists, or musicians. Think about the kind of people that you would like to live with. Who would share your values? Who would make harmonious housemates for your life? Who would inspire you to greater things in life? Make your life easier? There are a host of considerations when it comes to selecting the housemates that you want in your life. Think of it as a cross between family and friends—this is what your coliving partners will be to you and your life. In some cases it will be even better, because we can't select our family, but we can choose our housemates. Mindset is important in every aspect of life. We aspire to work with people who we can get along with. We should do that and more with the people we share a home with and it makes for such a perfect living environment when you obtain that. #LifestyleDesign

Five

Creation

A successful coliving space is composed of countless factors and priorities interlocking with one another in a harmonious fusion. When you get this right, it feels so good! Much of this outcome rests upon similarities between members in terms of both internal and external qualities. Remember that there is no single vision of how a coliving home has to be. The fiber of your space is modeled off of personal values. If you don't see any places that fit what you want, create it for yourself. There will always be others who share your thoughts and interests too.

Creation isn't too big a word for this. The start of the current coliving movement only happened a few short years ago. This is an industry (yes, we can call it that) that still needs to be shaped and formed. Unlike many parts of our life, there won't be one unifying manner of making a coliving experience work, but there will be a few core ideals that will help the rest of the coliving cohort sit up and take notice. There will be leaders here as there have been in the other big industries that have emerged over the last 20 years or so. Who will be the Mark Zuckerberg of coliving? Or the Jeff Bezos? Time will tell.

Mission & Vision
The idea of coliving is where everything else blooms from. Once you start on the right track with that goal of creating a coliving

community, then all of the other factors can be given the time and space to be explored and develop. You should look at this in two main ways: firstly, that you are creating somewhere to live, and secondly that this is a business. The reasons why this is the case will become obvious as you read through this book. So, let's get started first with your house mission and vision.

This is whatever you want to accomplish and create within your home. Keep in mind that you can create whatever you want to create. I know I've mentioned it before but I'm going to say it again, because this is where we're really going to dive into creating your vision, your mission, and your values that you want to set for your home and living environment.

Now first, let's get clarity on the difference between a vision and a mission statement because I know people get a little confused. A VISION statement focuses on tomorrow, and what your group wants to ultimately become. A MISSION statement focuses on today and what your group does to achieve it. Both are vital.

Let's start with your mission. This drives your home. It's what you do. It's the core of your home. It's your environment and objectives. And then also what it takes to reach those objectives. It shapes the culture of your home. So, what does your business (well, home in this case) do? For who? How? Again, is it entrepreneurs? Is it musicians? Is it artists? Is it conscious living? Is it vegans or vegetarians? A million different people have approached me with different concepts. So decide what works best for you and your tribe.

Then, what is that difference that you're contributing to in the lives of the residents that live there? Your housemates and the wonderful guests that visit? Or even the larger world? How will you impact your community that you live in, or on a global scale?

Our mission for Kindred Quarters is: **"To bring entrepreneurs together in a supportive and inspirational living community, and to build relationships with like-minded people."** Hopefully that example gives you an idea of where to start, but yours can be totally different.

Now for vision. Your vision statement gives your home direction. It's the future of your home, which then provides the purpose. What is the big goal that's only attainable in the long-term? What do you want to become as a home and a leader in your community? Kindred Quarters is the number one coliving company for entrepreneurs. What do you want your home to lead the way in? To be the most desirable for a specific group?

Now, your purpose. What is your purpose? What is your house's WHY? Why does it exist? What purpose does it serve? What cause does it support? Why are you guys existing together? This has to go beyond financial gain. If your only goal is to live rent free and make a bunch of money, then you might have a hard time. For reference, the purpose of Kindred Quarters is to provide an all-inclusive experience within a compatible coliving environment, enabling entrepreneurs to focus on what matters most: their business. Again, that's ours. That's what we live by and that's how we choose who gets to live with us, by that purpose-driven reason.

Let's discuss the name for your home. Of course, you guys can wait until you find the home and your housemates, and then come up with a name together. Maybe you want to make it an actual legitimate business, and have a logo and all that fun stuff, which you can easily do too. As you know, my company is called Kindred Quarters, but each home has its own name based on what the original housemates decide on. That's how we came up with the Entourage house in San Diego, the L.A. house is called the Hustle House. It's just fun to make it a group effort.

Come up with a FUN name for your home. One that conveys what you are all about. Aim to make it something fairly succinct, but also representative of the type of home this is and the interests it serves. In terms of marketing in the business world, there is always the search for something that sums up what a company stands for. A similar approach when naming a home is recommended. This can help it to be recognized by others who are searching for exactly what you're offering. As coliving expands in popularity, make sure this name will stand the test of time and remain prominent as more competing spaces arise. You will find this is an area of life that will expand rapidly over the next few years and beyond. Getting a name that represents all that is important to you now will help you to be grounded in your core values.

Aside from this, naming your place is a lot of fun. It lets you get all creative as a group of people and shows off the passion you have. Being part of a group is about identity. Your tribe is important to you as a person. Naming the place where that tribe hangs out can be just as positive and joyful. Branding is a buzzword in marketing that received far too much attention. It doesn't mean as much as 'branding experts' make it out to be. But it does fulfil an important role. I would suggest that you don't spend an inordinate amount of time on coming up with a name for your home. Think about what describes your space and run with it. If the name really doesn't work at all then you can change it at a later date. There are far more pressing matters to look into, as we will see over the course of this book.

I have to be honest. In my 15 years plus of being an entrepreneur, I've never seen a business leader become successful by having their number one goal of **making money** be their number one driver. Of course, that's still important and that keeps things alive but that should not be your actual purpose. That won't be enough to keep you going through the tough days. Just make sure you do have a deeper purpose. Actually, an amazing YouTube video on this topic to watch for more inspiration is a TedTalk called **Start with Why** by Simon Sinek.

Core Values

What will the residents of your home stand for and believe in?

For Kindred Quarters, these are ours:

Community
Integrity
Relationships
Support
Passion
Positivity
Kindness
Trust

Now for the most important part: How are you going to actually measure these results? So, for us, we like to look at how many positive reviews on Google and Facebook we can get as well as video testimonials from our current residents and the guests at our events. It's important for you guys to do the same.

It's especially valuable when they use our core value words in their testimonial without me coaching them to do that. It oozes authenticity. I just tell them to speak from the heart. Feel free to go to the Kindred Quarters YouTube channel to see the amazing testimonials people have already left us. People can really tell when testimonials feel real as opposed to scripted ones that you sometimes see.

When some of these keywords are said during the testimonial, that means you guys are nailing it. Right? Because you're not coaching them to say this stuff, just tell them to be honest. That's all I need you to do. That is truly a great way and measure for you guys to see if you're really hitting the vision, the mission, and the values of your home. If other people are able to articulate it well, it means you've gotten the message across in a real way.

Any type of project, business, or home needs a list of short term goals. They need to be specific, and they need to be measurable. Think about what you hope to do the next three months, six months, a year. Personally, I don't like thinking past a year because things this day and age are moving fast. However, many consultants or business coaches will tell you differently so you can try to do what feels most intuitive for you.

Even if house members align with one another in terms of mindset, they may not have the same idea of how they want a house to run. Some may be so focused on their work that their ideal flow of a home consists of minimal interaction and no sharing of ideas or recreational activities. However, others may see the social value of coliving first and put it before the allocation of work efficiency. Whichever these may be, it's important that housemates all agree on what it means to live in a space together. For example, why do you want to be a part of a coliving space? What does this arrangement mean to you? What does a day in the life of this home look like? It may be worth answering these questions for yourself and asking others the same to ensure that you're on the same page. You should all go into this discussion with the tenets of honesty and consideration. Not speaking your mind to protect the feelings of others will only leave you in a position where the things unsaid can cause an issue at a later date. Lay all of your cards on the table but make sure all of the discussion are positive.

It might feel odd that you are defining the characteristics of a house based on the people in it. But the simple truth of the matter is that, when modeled off certain values, the property will remain consistent even if one or more of the members leave. If you want to make a success of this, then you will look to the vision of the house as your guiding principle when it comes to moving on from people leaving. New recruits will fit into the vision because they believe, not because they want a place to stay. That sums up the difference between coliving and any other shared living space: the people want to be there because they believe in the vision that you have created. They are there because they believe what you believe. That not only creates a better place to live but enhances the life of people involved.

Values are the crucial element that will hold you all together when you are tired, under pressure at work, or feeling unwell. Knowing that the other people in the coliving collective are all pushing in the same direction as you brings a massive slice of comfort and keeps you going. It helps you to focus on the positive when there may be negative factors at play in your life. Being able to share your hopes and fears with others is an affirming part of being alive. Doing this with people who will understand you because they have similar experiences or a similar life view makes it even more worthwhile and effective. We all want these kinds of people in our life, but usually leave it up to chance that we will be able work with them or find the on the dating scene. Why not live with them? This doesn't just randomly fall into place very often so you need to take a little bit of control. Define what is important to you and then go out there and look for others that think the same way. Don't worry, we've added some advice in recruitment in this book too, as you would expect.

When considering what you want to accomplish & create with your home, remember that you can create whatever you want for your LIFE. What does this home mean to you? What are its goals? What potential impacts do you hope to make? For example, some coliving groups dedicate a portion of their collective efforts toward giving back by choosing an organization or pursuit that can help others. This may integrate the specific skills and resources that members of the home can offer, provided that all housemates share this desire and commitment. It's important that you define the long and short term aspirations for your space and potentially set goals to meet along with way. Although the specific implementation methods may undergo changes over time, your idea of a successful home and core aspirations will likely remain constant.

Treat all of this as though it is a long-term project, a business even. Thinking about your coliving space in these terms will allow you to build something that is far more than a simple place where people live for a period of time. It will become a home of shared hearts and minds that is a pleasure to be in. This comes from setting out what you want to achieve from the outset.

You can be and do anything you want in life. That's one of the things we are told as children all the time. But, the older we get, do we truly believe it? If we collectively work towards a positive and personal goal, then it can happen. Getting the support of others to achieve it is an amazing way of moving towards a goal. If you find others that want something similar to you, or the same, then you can collaborate to bring yourselves closer to that goal all the time. Don't think small with this one—dream big and then share it with others. They will want to help you get there. Their support is invaluable.

This should really appeal to your spirit of adventure! Making your coliving space anything you want it to be is a super exciting time in your life. Think about how you would have felt making a home of your own, with the people you want to spend time with when you were a kid! This is doing the same thing as an adult. There is the opportunity to make money from this if you are setting this up as a business and there is the opportunity to create an amazing living space for yourself and people you care about if this is something you are setting up as a home. Whichever your reason, the possibilities are truly endless.

There is so much to be said for just getting out there and doing something that nobody else does. That's one of the things that inspire others to create.

What Does all of This Mean?

That is at the end of the whole process of visualizing your coliving space: the meaning. If you are setting this up as a lifestyle choice or as a business, then you want all you do in life to have meaning. Pulling together all of these conceptual ideas before you take another step means you can have that reality check over what you are doing.

Does this make sense?
Am I doing things for the right reasons?
What does this mean to me?
What will it mean to others?
Does this translate well?
Can I make money from it?
Will it benefit my life?
Does it give me purpose?

I think asking yourself all of these questions at this stage can ensure you have that overarching 'why' that motivates you to get up in the morning and make things happen. Without that inspiration, you can end up not doing enough to push things in the right direction. And that's not where you want to be at all.

Six

Home

#LifeStyleDesign: Time to find the PERFECT Home

In order to make coliving a reality, obtaining the right space is of utmost importance. Without much real estate knowledge, this process may be daunting. Nowadays, there are countless valuable resources from which you can access the latest and most complete set of available properties. However, these useful outlets are not always fully recognized. Before looking, get a solid grasp of what you want in a home in terms of size, location, amenities, and layout. This will help to narrow your search as well as prevent you from making too many compromises in the process which can end up leaving you at a completely different place than where you began the search. Depending on whether the home in question plans to be rented or purchased, these options are valuable starting points to see what's out there.

The very first thing you need to establish is a budget. Looking extensively at a series of homes in a desirable area is heartwarming but doesn't get you any closer to results if you don't actually have the budget to secure a place in that area. Do your research before you set foot out the door and start searching. Get a realistic budget together with your fellow housemates, and from there you can determine the best place to live based on a range of factors. As with all of the advice in this book, it is especially relevant at the time you make a decision. A location that is suitable for the commute of all the people living there, or that has ample parking space for all the vehicles that will be parked there are probably good parameters when making this decision. Later on, if a coliving member moves out and you decide to replace them, then your new fellow resident will have to work to the rules, schedules, etc that are already in place. For now, work with what rolls best with you guys.

A home is defined in the eyes of many by two main things:

1. The feeling of light
2. The feeling of space

These are slightly different to the actualization of light and space. For instance, if you have a room that is factually large but filled with oversized furniture, then you wind up with a room that doesn't feel spacious. Again, you can have a room that has large windows, but if these are covered by large trees in the vicinity, then there is little feeling of light. During the winter months this can be even more accentuated. You can take a perfectly presentable room and make it feel less presentable if this is the case. Clever use of light will make a huge difference to how people feel when viewing, deciding and living in a coliving space. Be sensible with furniture (if you provide it) and with decoration. Keep it simple and keep it light.

There are some rooms that are more important than others when it comes to any home, and this stands just as tall with coliving spaces. It may surprise you that to many, it is the communal spaces that make the largest difference. The kitchen is now seen as the most important room in any home. This is where the socializing will happen. People will congregate there at meal times and discuss all manner of things. This should look and feel like an area where this can happen. The living room is another communal room that will need to fulfil the same function. Getting this to flow with the kitchen is the ideal you are looking for. People can then cook their food (more on whether this is done individually, as a group or by a professional chef later) and then take the conversation from there to the living or dining space and keep it up seamlessly. This is a huge attraction when you are putting people together that have a lot in common.

The way the home flows is another vital factor in making it a great place for you all to live. If you have to walk through one bedroom to get to another, for example, then this takes away privacy and makes the space less desirable. As you look at the possible places to live, make sure that all members of the unit get to view and take an active part in the decision. If some are just along for the ride, then you may find yourself in a position where you have to change decisions or find new people to share a space with you.

And don't forget the outside space. People always want a connection with the outdoors, pretty much all year round. This means you should consider a coliving property that allows this to happen. You will want to look for something that is low or no maintenance if possible. But the fellow housemates might want to put this in their budget to ensure that they have an outdoor place that looks great, is really functional and that they don't need to maintain themselves so a professional landscaper might be needed.

And all of these communal areas lead nicely back to the individual rooms that the coliving partners will occupy themselves. These may look and feel less important in the big picture, when you have the kitchen and other rooms to think about, but they can make or break the decision for someone to stay with you or not. Light and space are still important factors. But there are also a few other things you need to be aware of. Most people who chose to live a lifestyle that is conducive to coliving or being more mobile, typically do not own a lot of belongs. They are more minimalists so storage should not be a huge concern, however, can't hurt. This might be easier said than done with an existing building but there are always modifications that can be made.

In addition to storage, security will become a major factor in the decision to move someplace new. People want to know that they are with like-minded people, that's for sure. But they also want to know that they can trust the others they share a living space with. We look in a little more detail at security cameras in the smart home section of this book later, but for now, be aware that you will need to provide locks on doors for each personal room. This is good practice at any rate. Keys should be changed when someone leaves, so you might want to consider one of the newer systems where you can open the door via a code on a smartphone. These are much easier to change, especially at short notice.

How to Find the Right Home

You should start by deciding on the basics of what you're looking for. This includes how much you're willing to spend and the extent to which you're willing to make improvements on a place versus what you'd prefer to be pre-existing. At the same time, it's not always best to be extremely selective. For example, don't just start out looking for a big house. Although this direction can be great in plenty of respects, there are many other available options which can be easier to convert and better accommodate the staff that coliving spaces utilize. One alternative option is to consider searching for small hotels or villas which will already have many of the key layout components that you want. Of course, the size of the property that you're looking for will depend on the scale of your coliving space and how many people are expected to occupy it. You also need to think about whether the prospective place has proper room allocated for the communal areas, such as workspace and how distanced these shared spaces will be from personal bedrooms.

Let's not forget the most important part: bathrooms. Be sure to make sure there are enough bathrooms in the home. I would say no more than three rooms should share a single bathroom.

Another topic worth taking into account is parking. With a higher volume of people, where will cars be parked? Many locations do not have ample space to accommodate enough vehicles every day, so you may have to get creative.

We're sharing a few select options for kicking off this home searching process. A lot of the time, no single source lists every available place out there. For this reason, take your pick of these sources based on personal preference to get the best results. All are free to use, no need to have a real estate agent or broker help.

You will find that there are many resources available when it comes to looking for the best place to live. Ask around and put the word about that you are looking for somewhere to live. Use your contacts (and the contacts of your fellow housemates) to explore if there are any other opportunities out there. You might find properties being advertised independently on websites, notice boards or via word of mouth. The first step is to let others know what you are looking for. Once the word is out there, you will have some of the battle won. Nobody can read your mind and assume that you are looking for a place to live. So, get on the phone, post on your social media timeline, and start getting the ball rolling as soon as you can.

Craigslist
Although some mixed reviews may exist about personal success on Craigslist, it is certainly a high-traffic site that can provide you with the broad visibility of access desired. Craigslist is not something to fear outright. Since most people don't post homes for sale on this platform, it's particularly useful if you're seeking more of a short-term

housing option. Of course, this is best utilized as an initial starting point to learn about what's available, and then you can get in touch with the owner to find out the necessary details. Make sure you do some extra homework if you find a place on there that appeals to you, just to confirm that everything fits the description. This is one of the sites that is most used when looking for opportunities for a place to live. There will be different local versions, depending on the place you live, so look for local listings too and add power to your property search.

Hotpads

If you're pursuing the rental route, HotPads is a great place to go because it's specifically tailored to this type of housing search. Since this shows both houses and apartments for rent, you can review listings across the country at whichever level of detail is desired. For those who are particularly focused on finding a home in a specific area or relative proximity, the geographic map search style of HotPads allows you to do so easily. You can also benefit from the available pricing comparison and records of local schools to gain some perspective of the listing and area overall. HotPads is built for this exact scenario so check them out and consider all alternatives.

Don't ever settle for one or even two websites when looking for the ideal place to set up your coliving space. There are so many opportunities out there that you will want to explore more than one. Think about where the best opportunities to buy or rent a place exist in your chosen location. From there you will have the ideal places to get out there and research the market. Take a look at several options before making a final decision. If there are a few of you in the coliving collective then ensure everyone has the chance to look and add their opinion before the final decision is made.

Zillow
Use Zillow for a more all-around search tool that offers broad access to different properties and is used by both buyers and sellers. As a resource that covers both rental and sale listings, this is certainly promising if you're open to both of these options and don't want to limit your search. Zillow also ranges across all types of spaces, from apartments to single homes to clear land space and everywhere in between. In addition, you can get a lot of additional details such as statistical data, mortgage rates, and listing agents to contact by using this database. Zillow also provides estimates of the value of properties to give you a gauge as the consumer of how reasonable the pricing is. However, this more elaborate degree of information means that novice users may be discouraged or could use some assistance in order to use Zillow to its fullest.

Trulia
Similarly to the breadth of Zillow, Trulia spans across rental and sale spaces, as well as all types of construction. Both are also able to offer data on the markets being searched in order for the user to deduce whether the pricing is reasonable. Much of this info comes from the U.S. Census, so keep in mind that it may vary in complete accuracy based on how recently the past census was gathered. However, many would argue that Trulia is a bit more simple in terms of the variety of information offered and can be used on the phone through the App as well. It still provides the basics such as schools, maps, and crime rate reports to provide a rundown of each option. This can be favorable for first-timers who are more focused on searching for a home and don't want to address all parts of the process in this initial cursory stage.

MLS, then Skip Trace with Inquiso

MLS (Multi Listing Service) is the real estate tool of many real estate professionals in the field who can gain additional access to property details with solid accuracy. However, you do need to be a licensed real estate agent in order to gain access.

MLS encompasses mostly sale options but also some rentals, spanning across all residential property types including apartments, townhomes, duplexes, and single residences. However, many users often feel that MLS is better for sales than rentals, so keep this in mind depending on whether you plan to purchase.

There are always deals to be had when looking to buy a property and the foreclosure section of the MLS website could help you to find a real bargain for your coliving space. Remember there are certain rules relating to foreclosures dependent on the part of the United States you live in, so speak to your real estate agent to ensure you are doing things the right way. One of the crucial factors when buying a property is how motivated the seller is. This is often determined by how long the property has been on the market. This might put you in a much stronger negotiating position.

Negotiation with Owners

Once you've identified a space that passes your preliminary standards, it's time to get into contact with the property owner in order to move forward with the process. Of course, this will certainly vary based on whether you are entering into a rental agreement or going ahead with a purchase, the latter of which will likely need an agent to represent you in the process. Although buyers are not legally required to use a real estate agent in order to purchase a home, it's generally the best decision unless you already have an extensive background in the negotiation and contractual process.

If you or one of the others in your cohort have direct experience with this then you may want to employ their skills in this area. They could save you money by negotiating successfully with the owner of the property. Likewise, a real estate agent can negotiate on your behalf. If they are good at their job, then they could save you their fee and more by conducting the negotiation and gaining a great price for the property you have identified.

If you don't have experience here, then you should rely on the advice of a professional. There are a handful of things in this book that should be managed by a competent and qualified professional. The legal side of things is one of these. The fact that a property will probably set you back hundreds of thousands of dollars is a great reason to lean on the expertise of a professional in the real estate world.

One of the hardest parts is finding the homes and then getting the homeowners to agree to it. Although it can be challenging, I'm going to give you all the tools, tricks, and tips on how to make that possible. You definitely want to win them over.

First, it helps to communicate the benefits to these homeowners. So here are the big advantages to touch on:

1) The number one advantage for the homeowner is they are only going to deal with one person. You'll be the direct line of communication with them. They are not going to have five different roommates calling, texting, bothering them. This is big to them, most of these people are very busy and they won't want five different housemates calling them at different times. So that's the first benefit. They're dealing with one person who is responsible.

2) Benefit number two is that you will be willing to sign a long-term lease. Again, this is music to their ears because they don't want renters coming in and out every year. Let them know you'll do a 3-year, a 5-year, or even upwards of a 10-year lease depending on what you're comfortably prepared to enter into. For reference, I know that some coliving companies right now are signing 10-year leases. If the owner wants to, they can even build in increases if needed. This is a reasonable agreement that you two can discuss together.

3) The third and biggest benefit you need to communicate to them is the new industry of coliving. What that means is this is a very new industry, and if they can get in on the ground level, they'll be that much ahead of everybody else. The old-school property management companies are really going to struggle soon when other property homeowners are opening up to this new living model of coliving. Again, to get them excited, search on Google right in front of them. Show them how much funding is happening right now around the world globally in this new industry of coliving. Just stress all the perks and educate these people who may not fully understand how our world is shifting. Also educate them about the acronym HaaS: Housing as a Service.

Roughly speaking, it's likely that you're going to have a lot better luck with younger homeowners. Even if you don't have initial luck, do not get discouraged. I called 40 different people before finding the Los Angeles home. That's 40 "NO's!" I just told myself that if I hear this many "no's," it was bound to lead to a "YES." So don't get discouraged. Again, the more time that goes on, the easier it's going to get for you guys. It is the hardest part of your entire build-out of your home, but once you have it down, everything will fall into place, I promise.

It's also worth reaching out to any of your friends that are in real estate. Maybe they're property managers, sell real estate, or own property. These are your best people to talk to first because they already know and trust you, with your best interest in mind. Maybe they even have a property that they would love to get a renter in and only deal with one person.

If you're having a real challenge with owners and really love the property, other options exist. All of you can go on the lease together. If all the fellow housemates love the place too and are on board, that's your workaround. There are also some options if people don't qualify, whether credit-wise or income-wise, for the rent. They may have to put other people on the lease with them in order to qualify at all. Again, be open to that.

Part of the coliving appeal for some is the ability to be lease-free and to move in-and-out within 30 days notice. They want that freedom and flexibility, which is our model; but again, you can offer people the ability to go all in on it for six months.

The last point I will make is that you can offer what is called a "performance bond." That is something you're going to need to call your insurance agent to discuss, and they're not really too expensive. A performance bond is what you'll present to the homeowner and as something you're paying for with your insurance company. This essentially says to them that, if for any reason you default on the rent, they're covered. It's not customary, but a great worst-case scenario move. We will go heavy into insurances later on, but make a side note to consider this too if needed.

On Foot

One of the best ways to see what is happening in your neighborhood is to get out there and take a look. You might not get the same ease of use as you do on the internet, but you get a much better feel of an area if you walk the streets. It might give you a much smaller search area to look in, and this saves you vital time at the stage where you need to act quickly. Walking the beat will let you see the area from the ground level. It will give you a feel of what it will be like to live there. This is especially important if you are looking to set up a coliving space in a town or city that you are less familiar with.

Don't be afraid to try 'old school' techniques like this because they will pay dividends in the end. They are well used because they deliver results. We sometimes think that technological solutions are always the best. However, there's still a lot to be said about doing something the way it has been successful for decades or even longer. Leaning on pen and paper or walking on foot seem to be a dying art. Trust me, you don't always need to reinvent the wheel sometimes 'old school' tactics work the best.

Seven

Systems

Ready to set your home up for success? A smoothly operating coliving home does not arise automatically. It is the result of detailed planning, attention, and group consensus. You can achieve unparalleled coliving success by establishing beneficial systems for the home which mutually serve all residents. These systems can act as investments instead of expenses, provided that your group sees the value in each option and is willing to make their related costs a priority. There is so much to having a coliving space that works for all involved. There will be some give and take, but this needs to be grounded in a set of rules that exist and work for all of the people in the home. It isn't possible to please all of the people all of the time—that's just a fact of life. But it is possible to work together for the greater good. Think about the different elements of a coliving space that will contribute to its success, such as these.

Events

Events are a key point of appeal that coliving spaces offer. Key sources of networking are born from here. With the core of modern challenges centered around a need for outside input and diverse collaboration, the increased scope of this type of engagement is another unique benefit of coliving. When residents are committed to similar pursuits in business and progress, access to events is a key method for creating an interactive environment in which entrepreneurs or any like-minded group can advance their efforts and forge valuable relationships in the process. These can be specifically tailored to the broader goals of a coliving group, or loosely constructed and aimed at enhancing overall social bonds within the home. Positive events for coliving members can be work-specific, such as think tanks or masterminds seeking to pick the brains of others in the home who may be able to offer a fresh eye and perspective on tackling a problem. In coliving spaces where residents occupy varying skill sets, these think tank events can be particularly valuable as individuals may help to fill in the gaps where others may be lacking and vice versa. In addition, coliving members can expand their own personal knowledge and capacities through these events by learning the skills of others which can be applied to their own mental reserve. As a result, coliving adds an immeasurable monetary value to members by giving them actionable competencies which would likely require excess time and investment if anyone sought to acquire them elsewhere.

Socially speaking, coliving events also allow for a well-rounded experience and health of residents as they can detach from their work and participate in recreational activities to nourish the desire for play and connection that all humans have. This helps to foster a satisfied and mentally sound group of people who are as fulfilled in their personal life as they are professionally. Not surprisingly, allocating this time as a group to engage in new activities often transfers over to improvements in their own work, as individuals find themselves more inspired, invigorated, and wholly satisfied. These specific social events may vary in content based on the residents' hobbies, but can often be activities such as hikes, movies, meals, and guest speakers.

We will look in more detail later throughout the book at how to structure and plan events, but for now just remember how important they can be to the success of your coliving space and at least think about what you might do to make the events even more magical.

Hiring

You'll likely need to hire others to handle the tasks that the coliving home agrees to cover the costs for, and this process should be approached in the most efficient possible manner. Figure out a way to find the best applicants who are qualified for the positions you need filled. Your collective group can decide where to upload the job postings and how to approach the interview process. Since all housemates will benefit from these new team members, they should have some input on what specifications they are looking for and how the final decision is made. There will often be work needed in the space and you should all come together to complete the more basic elements such as simple repairs to a door handle, for instance. Taking control of a situation and delivering a solution is the most desirable way for each and every coliving member to be. This way you can all feel like you are working together for the same goal. If there are more pressing needs or something that has to be tackled by a professional, then you should work out who will hire the relevant tradesperson to do the work. There will be a strong network of people in and around the coliving people in your home. They will know people and might be able to find hires that can be relied upon and that could possibly offer a discount. This works in the favor of the whole living unit. If this isn't possible, then you should conduct research to find a reputable and reliable provider. The last thing you want is to find that you have chosen the wrong person and have to pay out a second time to put their work right.

We'll go further into building a network later on. But the elements in this section are ideally suited to someone who has (or is growing) a large network. They become a resource to ask questions when you need help, to lean on when you have a problem, or to recruit from when you need someone specific.

Shopping

It is quite likely that your coliving tribe will be so focused on their own activities that the need to shop for household supplies and necessities is lost as a priority. This is not necessarily a problem, as many alternative solutions can be applied. Shopping takes time, and time is not always easy to come by for many busy individuals. As a result, one way to organize shopping duties is by creating a circulating list in which each member takes turns doing it. This approach appeals to some people because it creates an equal distribution of responsibility across members with clear identification of who does the shopping at what time. Another solution is to identify one person in the home who volunteers or feels comfortable doing the shopping, and this additional effort can be rewarded or compensated in whichever way the collective home deems fitting. Or, if all coliving residents agree that none of them wish to take on the responsibility of shopping, they can enlist help by hiring another to do so. For example, the group can pay a chef to create meals for them who may be willing to do some of the ingredient shopping as well. You will want to be a team here, but make sure everyone pulls their own weight. It can end up with certain people doing all of the work and leaving others high and dry. If you need to make this part of your agreement, then get it in writing. Having groceries delivered is a great way to reduce the burden and let every part of the coliving unit make their own contribution to the list. Have a physical list around the home, preferably in the kitchen, and this can be updated as items run out. This might feel a little old school, but it is an effective and visual way of keeping track of what is needed. If there are items that are regularly on the list, then they can be added to a recurring grocery list either at a local store or with an online grocery delivery company. Knowing that you go through a bag of oranges per week will help you to establish that these items will be regularly delivered and ready for you to get on with your life with minimal fuss. It also prevents you from having to add the same items each week when they can be ordered automatically.

In addition, shopping must be addressed from the framework of whether members want to share food and household items or if they would rather be kept and used individually. This will also determine the fees required, and how to split these reasonably based on fair usage. This can be a potential area of concern and argument in a coliving space, so having rules for fair usage and cooperation from the outset will help to keep things running smoothly. This is about harmony and making sure you make life as easy as possible. The last thing you want is some petty disagreement over a food item to change the way people get on. Having like-minded people in the first place definitely reduces this risk, but having some set rules (that are easy to follow) will assist in this area.

Menus

The organization of a menu is directly linked to two extremely important components to success: time and health. When an individual lacks the time or personal wellness to do effective work, they cannot hope to advance or even remain consistent in their committed pursuits. By assembling a planned menu for residents of a coliving space, the stress of these essential elements is eliminated. Coliving residents can instead divert their attention to the magnitude of their work, and do it more effectively because the extra effort that most individuals must dedicate to this is no longer of the essence. For this reason, many coliving spaces may opt to hire a chef. Time is money, and it often proves more valuable for individuals to delegate these tasks to others who can be hired for this purpose. Although this is an additional expense, it is well worth the cost because self-care should not be ignored. Also, consider the proportional benefits gained in productivity which can far outweigh the monetary output. Part of success is knowing one's own strengths and weaknesses. If members of the coliving space recognize that cooking is not their strong suit, it is perfectly reasonable to outsource and assign this duty to another. Menus can be decided by the individual preferences of the coliving space. They can be pre-planned meals which the entire house agrees upon and eats together, or may also be individualized dishes for those with different dietary preferences or eating habits. As you all come together as a group of like-minded people, you will start to learn new things about each other. The kind of tea or coffee that each house member prefers, for instance, might be very different across the group. At first, people may not want to change their preferences or habits in this area. A particular brand or style of product might have come from years of use. But, as time goes by, people will naturally share and try each other's differences to come together. You might first try a certain drink with a fellow housemate and be totally converted to it. In most cases, these changes are for the better. Don't make your menu choices so all-encompassing that you have a series of narrow products for each member of your home. Try to look for common ground and try out some new things! Things like basic spices and foundational ingredients can be used for everyone.

It can be really easy to think that a menu system will cure all ills in terms of eating habits. But it won't completely. As with much of this book, you can't apply the rules too rigidly. If you tell everyone what they will be eating every night of the week then you may get some that won't want to participate. But if this is done in a much lighter way, then you can get consensus from the whole collective. Maybe a themed night with different options all prepared by your chef will keep more people happy at once than a single dish which may contain an ingredient that some don't like. Remember that there may be vegetarians or vegans in your collective, so the preparation of dishes becomes even more important. Keeping dishes clear of relevant allergens and avoiding cross-contamination will keep the entire household happy and healthy.

House Rules

The backbone of a thriving coliving space is concrete rules. These ensure that tribe members are all in agreement and there is no grey area which may lead to potential misunderstandings. Although certain values, practices, or concepts may seem obvious to one person, it cannot be assumed that this is the case for others. For this reason, it is always better to be as detailed as possible in order to eliminate any confusion. In doing so, there are countless questions to be answered when setting rules. The best way to deal with this is via a discussion and laying down the crucial elements of your living space.

Are animals permitted in the space? If so, which types are allowed and which are not? If certain animals are accepted, are they limited to specific rooms? Other topics to be answered are centered around guests. Can residents bring guests over to visit, and if so, at what times and where in the home? If guests are allowed overnight, how frequently is this acceptable? If overnight stays are fine, is there a point at which their consistency requires an additional payment to offset their use of the home (in terms of utilities, wear and tear, etc.)? What would this extra fee be? Sometimes, a solution to frequent overnight guests/partners in a member's room can incur an additional 20% cost.

These are all questions to think about and find an answer to that everyone can agree on. Another area of utmost importance is the realm of cleanliness. Decide if shoes can be worn in the house as well as how shared spaces such as some bathrooms, the living room, and the kitchen should be kept. Lay down specific parameters for the expected protocol if someone cooks a particularly smelly meal, or makes something which dirties multiple dishes that need to be washed. Usually, the best idea is to have each person remain accountable for the mess they produce. However, this is not always as simple because each person often adheres to a different time frame in which they believe to be sensible to complete this cleanup work. Some people are fine which getting to it in a few days, and others much prefer for it to be taken care of immediately. For this reason, it's best to stipulate a basic time frame within which residents should clear the space.

These guidelines may vary if your coliving home opts to hire outside help to maintain tidiness. You must also determine which sound volume is preferred in the space. This means setting 'quiet hours' when noise should be kept to a minimum. Noise also includes work and recreation—if a meeting is being held, be sure to do so in a place that doesn't distract others working or notify them in advance of your doing so.

When watching TV and movies, aim to use headphones, especially at particular times when it may be audible to others or just keep the volume to a reasonable level. It's also valuable to consider rules on personal property. Residents who share a bathroom must decide whether bath items are going to be kept in individuals' respective rooms, or if it's okay to keep them organized in the communal space.

This goes for things like electronics and valuables which may often be left in shared locations when not in use. Although for some this may be deemed perfectly fine, others could advise that they be stored in one's room to mitigate any potential issues of accidental damage or loss.

Once these rules are established, it's also important to consider how they will be implemented. For example, how will they be communicated to the new members? Generally speaking, it tends to be best to present new incoming housemates with these guidelines before they move in, so they can proceed while knowing the code of conduct and resulting consequences. Notifying new individuals of these rules is also a considerate option because this gives potential guests the ability to decline the opportunity if a distinct difference in lifestyle is apparent. After this, how will continuing residents be reminded of these rules? Printing and affixing clear physical lists of these rules in key visible spaces of the home are helpful to ensure that individuals do not forget specifics and can refer back to them if questions of clarification arise. On that note, what is the protocol if anybody breaks a rule? Depending on the coliving members and the nature of the issue, this response will be unique to each coliving environment because of course we are all adults.

Think big here. There is little point in sweating the small stuff initially because you could be there for months discussing all of the tiny details that might or might not even arise. Look at broad brushstrokes to begin with and build from there. Once the ground rules are in place, then you have a basis of respect to delve into any peculiarities. Get a core set of rules that must be signed up to and leave the rest to the spirit of the group, ensuring you have the right balance between freedom and structure.

Let's be realistic. Nobody really likes being told what to do. There is a common human resistance to rules, so you need to keep them as light as possible. Here at Kindred Quarters, we call them "Resident Commitments". We don't even call them rules.

Getting someone to sign up to 'Resident Commitments' will be a much easier sell than trying to get someone to sign up to a 58-page document filled with rules and regulations. The brain can't cope with that much information and the rules are less likely to be followed. You won't have achieved anything. This means you must break it down to the core principles of what you want the coliving space to look and feel like. These are the essential rules that will book everyone on this journey.

But the overarching message here is that people want to help. The goodness in others is the guiding light with all of this. If you have a set of guidelines and work on the principle that everyone wants a peaceful and happy existence, then you can't go wrong. The rules are there to pick up any confusion and weed out anyone disruptive. The rest of you can get on with your coliving experience in bliss!

Weekly Masterminds

My favorite part about what you create is how to have structure and form actual relationships where you connect with your fellow housemates on a deeper level. The best way to do this is with a Weekly Mastermind or meeting during which you all can find out what goals others have set, how far along they are, and what support they need. This is a great way to hold each other accountable and progress further in your own goals as well. It's also a nice designated time to reconnect with everyone and ask each other how their prior week has been. Even though you live together, you would be surprised at how rare it is that you are all together at the same time unless it's actually scheduled. It may be difficult to find a time that everyone is available in the same space at once, but just try to do what's most feasible.

Our meetings are every Monday night. One house does really structured Masterminds that are timed. The other house decided to do a more casual "family dinner" every Monday night. It includes a home-cooked meal that they all share and talk about how their week went and any other fun stuff. Clearly, there's some difference in how house residents choose to organize these meetings and the dynamic they have. Whatever you choose, just make sure it's most beneficial for those living in the home.

Another important creation part is to decide if you want to each visibly write your individual goals on a board in your home to really hold everyone accountable. Put your goals on a whiteboard. Put each person's name and their 1–3 different goals for that month. It could be business related, career, health, fitness, personal, or romance. Whatever they want and find most important at the time. You can also do a house challenge where the entire house sets a difficult goal together. By doing this, you are more motivated to get these things done because you're driven to complete them and attest to this success where everyone can see. Writing them down is also a great practice for manifestation because you'll see these goals every day when you walk past the board.

Eight

Team

Concierge & Chef

Another serious perk of coliving is the access to resources that can make your life so much easier. With a large amount of people in the space, it also makes sense that this additional help exists in order to simplify the process of coexisting with multiple others. Primarily, a concierge is one of the ways that coliving homes are able to streamline operations in terms of the volume of visitors, events, and meeting that are bound to occur. This removes much of the extraneous time that residents spend organizing their schedules, which could be better spent elsewhere at work in their areas of expertise. Think about this in terms of the money you could earn in the time saved rather than as an expense. Time is that precious commodity that we just cannot make more of so we should protect it at all costs. Hiring a quality concierge will help pull everything together from a group of people that are all living together but live potentially diverse lifestyles. Think about all of the tasks a concierge could fulfil for your coliving home. Having someone there to welcome visitors, be there for any deliveries or workmen and provide the glue that keeps the whole coliving space together is pretty much an essential.

The same goes for hiring a chef. This may seem like a luxury, but the distribution of cost across multiple housemates as well as realistic consideration of time value makes it clear that these amenities are not only cost effective at the end, but also contribute to an efficiently organized lifestyle. It is important that coliving members agree upon hiring this team, as it is difficult to create a system in which those who opt out are actually separate from the resulting benefits. You would think that hiring a chef for your own home would be a cost too far. But divide that cost by the number of people in your coliving space and you might find that it is well within your means. Of course, you will need to discuss this with the rest of your housemates, but the prospect of having your meals cooked by a professional will most probably be too great an opportunity to miss out on. This goes for a whole host of professions that you might consider.

If the property has gardens, then getting a rotation together to get people to contribute to their proportion of the upkeep could become a logistical nightmare. Getting a gardener in once per week in the summer and at other times throughout the year could be a much better way of managing this. The same might go for a handyman for all the work that needs to be carried out around the property. Basic maintenance will protect the value of the home, especially important if you have bought, and keep the landlord happy—a great reason for those who have chosen the rental route. Whichever hires you decide are important for your living space, make sure you have the agreement of all people involved before you set out on the next step of the journey—actually going out there and hiring.

There may be other hires that you want as the coliving experience develops and the collective see different priorities. This is just a case of communication, getting buy-in from others and moving forward with the same principles you have already used when recruiting in the past. Don't think that the initial idea is the only one you can have in terms of who you guys get working for you. Think about what the lives of the people who occupy need and suggest accordingly.

How to Hire

Get to know exactly what you want from the people you will hire. If the majority of the coliving occupants are out at work until 7pm every evening, then hiring someone that finishes at 5pm doesn't fit the bill. Although new housemates may come and go, you must make decisions based on the interests of the people present when you hire. Finding hires that are flexible will help you adapt in the future, but the best person for the job at that moment in time will be the overriding factor when making a decision. As with hiring anyone, you will need to do your research. Getting references and looking back at their work history will help you make that decision. When moving to the interview stage you have two main choices: select one or two members of the coliving home to make a decision on behalf of all, or get as many people as possible involved so you have a consensus decision. Reaching consensus in these situations is notoriously difficult, so we suggest the first approach for the best chance of success.

How to hire is a complex subject. There are blogs all over the internet written by recruitment specialists and all other manner of people suggesting how to best recruit others. But the fact of the matter is that this plethora of information can often add to the confusion. Think simply when you recruit. Decide who you want, what you want them to do and how you want them to be. From there you should have a better recruitment journey than if you didn't plan ahead at all and definitely go off your gut and intuition.

Interview

The interview process is a vitally important part of getting the right person for your coliving home. The steps that come before this include defining who you want and what you want them to do. From there you can narrow the field of candidates and invite the select few to interview.

You have a couple of choices for where to interview candidates and the selection will depend on how you all feel about letting someone into your home. You could interview there or in a neutral venue such as a coffee shop or restaurant. It may be a more relaxed and informal thing if you meet at a local cafe because there feels like less pressure on the potential hire to adapt to the situation. You will get a good feel of how they are as a person, and that's arguably just as important as their qualifications or experience. Of course, if you are looking for a chef then you want someone who has done this before, preferably in a domestic environment. Especially since this person will be spending a good chunk of time in your new coliving space, you want to know what they are like as a person. If there is going to be more than one interview steps then you may want to conduct the initial one in a neutral venue before moving on to the home space for something a little more formal. The number of housemates in the first one could be limited where the second will open up the opportunity for everyone to meet the potential hire and vice versa.

As with so much of the advice in this book, you need to think about this in terms of a business. Whether you have a coliving space that you share with a few friends, or you are making this your business, the principle of treating this like a business still stands. The collective of friends don't want to fall out over the financial side of things, which is an essential part of the coliving experience. In terms of interview, there should be a formal element to it. You want to know that your hires are fit to carry out the task you assign them. The fact that you can come together and spread the cost over a number of different people doesn't detract from the fact that you are spending serious money here. And the people you do choose to hire will be grateful that you have treated them in a professional manner. It will make them more loyal in the future then if they feel like they are being treated casually and their work doesn't really mean a lot to you guys.

Training

You will want the people you hire to stay at the cutting edge of their profession, so it might be reasonable to get them the relevant training. For example, if there are changes in food hygiene regulations, you would want your chef to be right on top of that to keep them compliant and protect all of the people in the coliving home. Think of this in very much the same vein as an employer-employee relationship. You have a responsibility to ensure that your hires are in the best possible shape to look after you all. In addition, there might be other things that you would want from a hire that they don't already have. Again, we will use the example of a chef. You could as a group decide that you want them to pick up a specialty in Chinese food if it's your favorite. In this case, a course in professional Chinese cooking classes will benefit the chef and the whole coliving home. As with so much of the coliving experience, spreading the cost among the group means that your money can go a lot further. The collective mindset of a coliving group is that they share resources, ideas and experiences. That's why you look for like-minded people from the very start. You will all work together to a shared goal.

Nine

Legal Fun

Starting a business as a coliving entrepreneur is fun. You can make money by providing exciting and engaging places to live for others. Even if you start a coliving space as a group of people (a collective) then you will have a business on your hands. With all of the fun, you need to consider the legal aspect of this.

You may think that the legal side of things would be an afterthought. You would be wrong. Getting this wrong can land you in a whole heap of trouble and leave your coliving idea in the gutter. Don't ever think that you can sort this out later. It is real and will be staring you in the face every day if you don't have a set of solutions in place.

As with any business, you must look into the legal implications if something goes wrong. Making sure you are in a good place for that eventuality, no matter how obscure it might sound, is good business practice. Here are some of the areas you will want to consider before embarking on this amazing journey.

Insurances (Business, Liability & Renters Insurance)
Treating your coliving space with the keen eye of a business person is one of the key elements that will keep everyone safe and protected. And that protection is one of the key principles of coliving. Insurance might not feel like it's connected with the inspiring place you are trying to create. When you think of a group of like-minded

people living in a harmonious place, the word 'insurance' doesn't automatically come to mind. But it should.

A coliving business should have business insurance. It's as simple as that. All of the risk factors for any business are also present in a coliving business. You should be able to provide protection for yourself, your housemates, your employees, and any members of the general public that come into contact with your coliving home.

Liability insurance covers you against third party claims. It's the insurance that gives you peace of mind so you can rest in bed at night. If someone claims that they have been financially or otherwise affected by the actions of your business, then you may very well face a claim from them. In this instance, you want to be in a position to fight your corner. Without liability insurance, the liability will actually fall on the business, which essentially puts all of the pressure on you to act. A quality liability insurance will not cost a massive amount of money but is worth every penny to you. It puts that legal barrier between the coliving home and a potential claim. If you select the right policy, then you will have access to legal advice and someone who can defend you in a court of law if the claim comes to that point.

Having someone to lean on in this instance is worth its weight in gold. You can trust that you are being represented by a legal professional who is charged with looking after your best interests, and not have to pay for this privilege out of your own pocket directly.

Renters insurance helps to look after your belongings when renting out a space to someone in your coliving home. If you have space to rent out to others, then this will often also include your belongings such as furniture, carpets, drapes, sometimes electrical appliances, and others. The shared spaces are just as important as the bedrooms your renters will occupy. These are usually filled with the conveniences of modern life. Some of these might include the technology that we'll look at in a later part of this book. If an unscrupulous or aggrieved housemate decides to leave and either takes or damages some of these items, then you'll need some form of proof, like photos, in order to replace them. Likewise, accidents will happen in a home of many people so there might be belongings that wind up damaged or useless. In this instance, your renters' insurance will be on hand for you to make a claim. There will usually be an excess on these policies and they often don't cover wear and tear, but they do provide essential protection against some of the potential large costs that might come about from renting out space in your coliving community.

Company Incorporation

A business that makes money from a coliving space should seriously consider becoming incorporated as a company. This means that the business is structured in a different way, and one of the main advantages of incorporation is that you as an owner have limited personal liability in the event of a lawsuit. We looked above at the potential need for liability insurance in the event of a claim or lawsuit against the coliving home. If you incorporate the business, then you become a shareholder and essentially a different legal entity to the business itself. Your personal protection goes up.

There are costs associated with incorporating a business and it takes a little time to get the legal framework and structures in the right place. A legal professional or a professional company formation agent are your best bets to get this show on the road. Getting all of your ducks in a row with this is the best way forward. Go over all of the advice in this book regarding the legal processes and ask a lawyer to look into anything that you feel is relevant to you and your coliving business. This way, you can get full legal service in one hit rather than piece by piece as you think of things. Doing it all with one trusted adviser will mean you get all the advice up front and it might even save you on costs because they are working for you on a range of things all at once. Speak to your legal representative. If you haven't used one before for specialist business advice, then seek recommendations from people you know and trust.

This is a business. If you treat it like one, then it has the potential to look after you in return. If you treat it like a hobby, then it will pay you like a hobby—and potentially expose you to a collection of issues so be sure to stay on the ball when it comes to covering your legal you-know-what.

Employment Contracts

If you have people working for you in the coliving home, then you generate responsibilities towards them in terms of their employment. The same as you working for someone else, you want a structured employment contract with all the relevant rights and responsibilities outlined for all to be able to refer to. Becoming an employer means you have to look after those that work for you. This can include training and certifications, annual leave, and reliable procedures in the event that you want to part ways and move on. If you employ someone then you have a need for that person. Allowing them to walk away without any notice period can leave you in a pickle so ensure that things like this are written into the agreement. It gives both sides the protection that they rightfully look for in an employer-employee relationship.

There may be people that are absolutely essential to the smooth running of your coliving space, so offer them the kind of salary, perks, and contract that they would look for on the open market. If you want to optimize your coliving business, then you need to hire high quality people that will provide the best experience possible for those living in the space. Figure out budgets and make sure that these cover all the expenses of taking on an employee.

1099 Agreements & Independent Contractors

Similarly, if you are hiring people on a contractor basis, there is a legal document that provides cover for both parties, known as a 1099 agreement. It defines many of the areas that are important to outline when getting contractors to work with you. It lays out the scope of the work you want carried out, the amount of time you want this done for, the compensation agreed by the two parties, and can also go into further detail so you and the contractor know exactly what's required. It even gives details of what to do in the event that the work isn't of a satisfactory standard. In other words, it clearly states what you want them to do and what they get in return. From their point of view, it also details what they don't do as well as what they will do.

Sometimes you may want a contractor to do something a little extra or different to what they have already agreed upon. This can lead to dangerous ground and needs to be covered from the outset. Hiring a contractor because they are excellent at one thing doesn't necessarily follow that they can carry out other tasks. If you want something else carried out then you should ask or look again at the market for the best practitioner. As with any hires you go for, do your research and select the one that works best for you. Look at value for money and quality of work over price to ensure you provide the best coliving space you possibly can for the people who live in your space or spaces.

Vendor Agreements

You'll have a series of people who supply things to you throughout the course of your coliving business and you should look for value and service with each of these. Items that you buy on a one-off or irregular basis such as furniture might need to be conducted on an individual transaction basis. But there may be certain items that you buy regularly. If you or your coliving home get products on a monthly or weekly basis, then a vendor agreement with a specific seller can add a great deal of protection to the buying process. If you want them delivered at a set time on a specific day of the month at a set price, then a vendor agreement is the ideal way to make this happen. You and the vendor know exactly where you stand. This means that you have a point of reference if something goes wrong such as a late delivery or the quality of the products not being up to the required standard. As you build better relationships with suppliers (and potentially build the business with more coliving spaces), then you will be able to look at savings costs here. But in the first instance, the focus will very much be on getting the best service for the people who live in your space.

These agreements clear up everything. That's the position you want to be in. Don't slow down and let things slide. That is a route away from success.

Shareholder Agreements

The way that you set up a coliving space might necessitate different agreements and contracts. Buying is different from renting. Having all the housemates as part of the ownership is very different from having one or two owners and renting out the rest of the space. If there is more than one party to the ownership, then a shareholder agreement is a pretty vital piece of paper. People go into business with friends and family all the time. And everyone walks into that situation with the best of intentions. They don't envision any issues in their shared future. But people fall out, families fall out, friends fall out. And this can cause a major issue when you all share a business. It can lead to arguments and legal wrangles. This costs big money to resolve and nobody ever really wins. A shareholder agreement sorts all of this out from the start. It will include clauses on what to do if there are any disputes, voting rights, and the conditions under which you would sell your share or the whole business. Sorting all of this out before you get into the business might feel like a cost that you can't stand in the short term. Organizing from the beginning clears up any confusion in the end—that's where the real costs could come in if you are not in the right place.

The shareholders of any company should be in a position to leave if they wish to. Financial circumstances mean that any one of the shareholders might need access to the cash they have invested or part of it. If there is a set procedure for making this happen, then all can rest assured that their investment is as liquid as possible. Some opt to offer the opportunity to the other shareholders before opening it up to existing coliving members who are not shareholders, then for sale on the open market. Whatever route you decide, it is best for all concerned if this is set in writing from the very start so there are no gray areas.

Real Estate Lease/Acquisition Agreements

Lease/acquisition agreements can work in one of two ways in relation to coliving and both could be important to ensure that everyone is looked after in this situation. Whether you are an owner or a renter, there will be some occasions where a lease/acquisition agreement is relevant. A real estate lease/acquisition agreement allows someone who has been renting a place (or part of a place) to be gain automatic rights to buy into it at some stage in the future. It has been used by landlords to warm up tenants to buy from them in the future once both parties are happy with the living arrangement. It's a slightly more complicated structure with coliving, since the whole property is likely not being offered, but rather a share in it would be on the table in this instance.

One of the methods for attracting tenants to your property is that you may want to offer them the opportunity to become something more than a tenant in the future. Lots of people want somewhere more concrete to live and call their home. In the modern world of restricted finance and increasing property prices, this isn't always viable and certainly isn't always attractive to others. But owning a share in something that they feel at home in and want to call their own might be a much more attractive proposition for many. So offering this at some stage in the future for your prospective residents can be a great recruitment tool. You want people who believe in what you stand for. This will get those people as a more permanent fixture rather than just passing through. You want people who live the same values as the rest of the unit. If you can offer these people the chance to buy in, then you will find that they treat the place better, make more of an effort, and become a vital part of your coliving experience because there is a grounded sense of attachment.

As a renter in a coliving home, you'll want the same opportunity for yourself. Look for these if it is something that appeals to you. This can be the perfect way to get on the ladder and become part of the coliving lifestyle in a bigger way than just a renter. You may want to keep your options open initially and a lease/acquisition agreement is a fantastic way to do just this.

The second way that a real estate lease/acquisition agreement might be part of a coliving business is if you rent a place with one eye on buying in the future. If you are very new to this, then you might have a few reservations about how it might all pan out in the future. Although I recommend that you commit to this fully, it's totally understandable that you might have a few doubts. One way of easing these doubts is to try before you buy with a lease agreement that can be converted to purchase at some stage in the future. These agreements are commonplace and, as with all of the advice in this section, you should speak to an independent legal representative to make sure that you understand what you're agreeing to before signing on the dotted line.

Zoning Laws

Properties are zoned to dictate the type of usage permitted for a given space (commercial, residential, industrial, etc.). Be careful to ensure that the space you choose to live in is zoned properly for the residents occupying it and the type of work they may be doing out of the home. Many of the people involved in the coliving market at this moment in time work from their home and wouldn't want to find out that they are breaking any codes or laws.

If you are the business owner then it's your responsibility to look after them, their rights, and their businesses. It could end up with them moving out with little or no notice, closing their business down, or receiving a fine or caution depending on the area you live in. That's the last thing you want for the people under your care. This should be checked thoroughly to make sure you don't fall foul of any laws and end up in trouble with the authorities. It's a pretty simple check to look after yourself and the people who will live with you. There are certain zones and they are set up for a reason. You wouldn't want to set up a home in an industrially zoned area, as an example. If you are not sure, then ask a legal professional to look into this, preferably one with a background in real estate development.

Public Liability

There will most probably be a strong need for public liability insurance in the coliving world. There are a number of risks involved with coliving, especially as there will be people in and out of the space on regular basis to visit friends, carry out work and even the times when you are looking for new coliving members. You want everyone to be covered and looked after when they step foot inside your home. This means you will have to seriously look into the need for public liability because many of the people visiting the home will be just that: The public, especially there is coworking involved.

If someone unfortunately gets injured when in your home, then one eventuality is that they may look for some form of financial redress for their injuries. Unless you want this money to come out of the pockets of the people living there, then you'll need liability insurance. The amount will depend on the size of the building, but one with a high cover and low excess is the perfect choice. This shouldn't cost too much and can be picked up for a few dollars per month if you find the right provider. Look at this when speaking to your legal representative at other areas of legal practice as they will have experience in advising clients as to the best policy for them. Rely on the experts when it comes to matters like this because a cheap policy might not provide the coverage you need. Unfortunately, it's often the case that the best test of an insurance policy is when you need to make a claim. Don't wait that long to find out. Rely on an expert.

Eviction of a Housemate or Guest

Although it is everyone's hope that the issue of eviction will never arise, this possibility must be still planned for regardless. If a housemate continues to break the rules which were clearly outlined for them (or whichever unanimous grounds for eviction the home agrees on), this process is the next step. The first place you protect yourselves in this regard is with the housemate agreement at the very beginning. Think about how you can make this fair, inclusive, and airtight if needed. A legal document should be drawn up by a lawyer, so consult a reputable one to give you something that will stand up if you ever need it. As time goes by, you'll find other issues that may need to be addressed here, so communicate this and get them added with a regular review.

We want to live in an issue-free world where everyone gets along. But this just isn't possible if we take a look at the reality in front of us. Sometimes we just have to accept what the world is like. There may very well be, for whatever reason, the potential for moving someone on, possibly against their will. You should have the eviction procedures outlined in the agreement that people sign when they become involved in the coliving space. If this is a renter, it would be easier to enact than if you ever came to the position where you needed to evict a shareholder or co-owner. In either case, rely on professionals to help you get everything sorted with minimal fuss and within the laws of the land. Seek legal advice, follow the rules you are given, and get someone else to enact the eviction. There may be a small cost associated with this but it sure beats having to remove someone yourself. This can get messy and you want to stay safe at all times. Try to keep everything amicable (maybe think about how you have gently and seamlessly broken up relationships in the past and take the best of these) and you'll see the best results this way.

Let's not dress this up in any other way. Evicting someone from their home is an undesirable experience for everyone involved. The person you are evicting may have an issue that has prevented them from being part of the group or paying their rent. Never forget that this is another human being and they are just probably not a great fit for the rest of the home rather than them being a bad person. Creating the best for others should be one of the reasons you start your coliving journey, so don't forget this if things become a little tense. Treat everyone with the care and compassion that you would want, and you'll see the bigger picture at all times.

Ten

Giving Back

One of the real pluses of being involved in the coliving community is the ways you can connect and engage with others. Once you have set up your coliving space and been situated in it successfully for a period of time, you will likely want to help others achieve exactly what you have. As you set up, you might have spoken to a number of others on the subject to get ideas, ask questions, and learn best practices. And this is all part being a member of the coliving community. Once you become a part of it, you'll never want to leave!

Coliving changes the way you view your life. But, you may have started out with a lot of questions to get your head in the right place. As a new way of life that you hadn't experienced before, maybe you needed a little persuasion to get to where you are now. Consider that others might be in exactly the same situation.

This is one of the reasons I put this book together. I want to give back to the community. There are many people out there that can benefit hugely from coliving, so I want them to learn all there is to know about it. Without the information in this book, people might have a stack of additional questions about how they can make this work for themselves and the people around them. There are many ways in which you can spread the word.

Mentoring

That is where something like mentoring comes in. You can become a part of the wider community and help others on their coliving journey by being a mentor to them. This is a simple way to provide support.

Think about how you can deliver this. There are many ways to start conversations with people in order to help them understand coliving and put it into motion for the benefit of their life. If you are an online fan, then there are forums and chat rooms where people may be asking about coliving and how it can work for them. Websites such as Quora are always filled with questions about every subject under the sun. Coliving is definitely one of these. It's always helpful to spread the word and let people know about the experience you've had with coliving. There is also a duty to mention anything relevant that might not readily be viewed as a benefit or positive. If there are zoning issues or problems removing a tenant, like the ones we've discussed earlier in this book, then don't be afraid to mention these either. But be sure to follow this up with sound and practical advice on how to ensure that these potential issues can be avoided. All great things have risks and kinks to work out. Point them to this book as well, as it contains a vast amount of information that will help people to set things up in the right way.

But having an online presence is one thing. Actually providing mentoring in your town or city is something else altogether. Something that feels like it has a far greater value. There are always people near you that can benefit from coliving in a massive way. Some already know about it and don't know how to approach the process. Some don't even realize that it's a thing. Giving back to the world is a satisfying place to be, so look for those that want to start their own coliving experience and offer your support.

You can find people who have placed advertisements online and offline as well as people who are looking to link up with others in their living arrangements. Once you have identified people who are on the journey, you can make contact with them. I suggest that you let them know a little bit about your story, ask if they need help, and offer to meet them in a friendly public place. Your safety is paramount in all of this, so make sure you stay safe and meet somewhere neutral just to be sure. Once you have built up a rapport with someone, then you can move on to letting them see your coliving space and what that entails.

You'll already know that anyone on the early part of the move from traditional living to coliving will have a whole heap of questions. They will want to know what it is all about, what it feels like, and what the potential pitfalls are. You have all of this information from experience. You can help them fill in the blanks. I'd suggest that you make a mentoring relationship something longer term rather than a quick meeting. You will gain a lot more fulfilment from this and the person you are mentoring will get so much more from it too.

This is a win–win situation. You get to spend time talking to someone about a subject that is close to your heart. You get to share that passion with someone who is likely just as excited as you. And they have you to listen to their thoughts and provide advice that they can't really get in many places. Think about it. The way that most people live means that there isn't a great deal of advice on this subject. You can become a guru in this field and help others to become what they want to be.

All of this, though, is reactive. It's looking at the actions of others and responding. To really make a difference in your community, you might have to consider being much more proactive than this. You might have to go out there and let people know what coliving is and how it can benefit their life. Think about the kind of people that might look into this as a way of life. You might want to target business groups, employers, graduates, or any other organization where people looking for a better way of living might congregate. This can be a similar research effort to the one you used when identifying potential coliving partners at the start of your journey. Now this includes looking for people who can benefit from coliving, but that don't know anything yet (or enough) about the phenomenon to make a decision.

If this is the kind of mentoring that floats your boat, then you need to find an outlet for this. Meeting people who want to hear about coliving and what it means for them may not be an easy task. So, you should think about this like a business proposition. Decide where you can engage with others and put your knowledge and experience to good use.

Business networking groups are a great way to meet new people and expand your network. With the best business networking, you don't just get to speak to the people in the room—what you are in fact doing is accessing their contacts as well. Talk about coliving and your experience and let them know that you are looking to help like-minded people on the same journey. Everyone will know people in their circle that would consider or benefit from coliving, but you just have to jog their memory. They say that the average person knows around a thousand people. So when they stand up, imagine a line of a thousand people standing behind them. These are the people that you would like to speak to, in addition to anyone suitable in the room. Remember that this isn't a hard sell—you are looking to help people!

You might find some joy with real estate agents who speak to people looking for somewhere to live on a daily basis, or even mortgage brokers who will often do the same. Their life consists of being in and around property and those looking to start a new life in a new place. They may come across people who are looking to do the same thing as you, or who are ideally suited to the coliving lifestyle. You could ask them to connect you with these people in order to give some mentoring. You will get the satisfaction of supporting someone who wants and needs a little guidance.

There are, of course, other ways to connect with people in your local community and engage with them while offering your mentoring services. Think about how this might work for you and you'll see the chances to share your experience and the knowledge you have built up over time. There will be good and bad things you have encountered, and both are valuable as you seek to support someone on an exciting similar journey.

Community Outreach
Connecting to your local community is another great way to give something back. We'd better start with a definition:

> Community Outreach is the concept of providing services to people who may not ordinarily have access to those services. Think about this. There may be people in your community that need the skills that the people in your coliving group possess. What better way to make the lives of other people better than to group together and help others?

For example, if your group consists of artists and musicians (I know this is kind of a random choice, but the coliving lifestyle suits these groups) then teaching others how to paint or how to play a musical instrument can add a lot of value to their life. Being able to help others in the name of your coliving space will help gain some publicity too, which is also useful to expand or recruit new housemates as well as helping others to develop a new skill or feel better about their lives. Even if it's only to escape for a few hours a week from whatever their lives normally look like, this small act has a massive value for many people.

You can explore community outreach groups in your area to see what connections and synergy there might be. The organizers will help you understand what they are looking for and how your skills, time, and expertise can benefit others. These are typically helpful for the elderly, charities, and young groups. In big business, they talk about Corporate Social Responsibility, or CSR, as this covers the ways they engage with their suppliers and the community in which they operate. In very much the same way, you want to reach out to your community and show that you care. There is no need to have a CSR policy like a massive organization such as Starbucks, for example, but keeping an eye on the community you live in is a sure way to keep grounded and contribute something to the world.

Donating Money

For many people, the traditional view of giving back to society still stands as the most important one: giving money to people in need. There are several ways of doing this as a coliving tribe where you might opt to give cash instead of time, skills, and experience. And that's totally fine too. It will help you to support people locally if you do it in the right way.

You may want to select one or more local charities and give them a donation every month, quarter, or year. Maybe a certain proportion of the rental payment you take from people could be earmarked for charity. Or, you can choose to have specific events geared toward that charity. Having a set way of raising money and supporting your chosen charity is going to mean that you don't forget and let life get in the way. If you want to support a charity then make it public, get it planned, and make it happen.

But you also don't have to rely on others to set up a charity. If you feel strongly about something in your community (and that you feel it isn't being covered by anyone else), then go ahead and start your own charity. There will be some work involved with this, but it can be very rewarding in the end. Like above, you'll need some set ways of raising money for the charity and want it to be as supportive as possible for your chosen cause. Being as specific as possible with the reason you have set up a charity will help you to raise money and target where it needs to be. This is a great way to give back to the community you live in. There may be specific projects you want to see happen or you might want to focus on support for housing, considering that the coliving arrangement has brought you here.

Making Space Available

One of the most direct ways you can make a difference is with the property you live in. There are many people out there looking for a decent place to stay anywhere from a few days to a few weeks or months. If you have some spare space in your coliving property, then you might choose to offer it to these people and help them out.

Obviously, this is your home and the home of others, so you don't have to open the space to just anyone at any time, but think about any occasions when your property might have spare capacity for someone in need of a little help and can access what you have. Space can be at a premium in large cities and near large employers, so think about what this might open up in terms of opportunity. These people may not be able to pay you as much, but they can share their experience with you on social media, by way of a blog or word of mouth. Any of these help the standing of your coliving space in the local community and provide great press. As we are all about giving back, this is vitally important. We are what we leave behind in this life. If we can spread a little joy and happiness to people who really need it, then we are fulfilling our goals.

Speak to local charities to see who needs help with this and what you can do to provide it. You may want some form of guarantee from the charity or might even decide to carry out your own referencing, but whatever you do, make sure your people are safe. You have a responsibility to look after the people in your home, the same way as a hotel. We've already outlined the fact you need to look into public liability insurance and the like. So looking after your people is an integral part of this.

Whatever you decide is a great way of giving something back, be sure to back it to the hilt. Doing something in a half-hearted manner doesn't bring the right results. I always suggest that you put your heart and soul into anything you do. Your living space is such an important part of your life that you should take this philosophy with you on that part of the journey too. If you feel strongly about something as vital to your existence as your home, then this is a wonderful feeling. Spread the word! Speak to as many people about this positive piece of your personal jigsaw as you can.

Eleven

Events

Expanding Your Network Exponentially

Your network says a lot about who you are as a person. They say that the average person knows around a thousand people. Imagine a line of a thousand people stood up behind everyone you knew. This is quite a powerful image. This is their network, and, by proxy, can become your network too. So you should think about how you can make connections in these networks. It will help you to build your list of people who might be interested in coliving. You will probably find that once you have started on this journey, you will want to bring the joy of coliving into the lives of as many relevant people as possible. This can only be enabled if you widen your net. The best people to live in the coliving spaces you create are those that you already have a relationship with. It won't stop the need to carry out referencing or anything like that, but it will give you a good head start in looking for people that you know, like, and trust.

Events are a fantastic way to meet people and showcase the amazing place you have created. Inviting people into your home is such an amazing way to connect with people on a more personal level. Think about all of the connections you can make and what they will mean to you personally and your coliving home.

An event can be anything from a few drinks to a business networking meeting or a more formal dinner. Even looking at interesting things based on the people in your coliving space will generate interest, spread the good word, and help people to learn about coliving and what it might mean to them. Imagine that the next time you open another coliving space or need to find another house member, you don't need even to advertise because you already have perfect people lined up. This can be the awesome power unlocked by hosting an event and getting people connected to what you do and what you can do for them.

Thinking about your event, you'll need to go through several steps to make sure it does all you want it to do. As with anything in life, planning makes it all easier. So, here are the essential steps to making an event go smoothly and achieve the objectives you want.

Pre-Event
Before the event, you should take some time to understand exactly what it is you want to achieve from your time and effort—and your cash. There are very few events that don't take up one or more of these. And there is nothing wrong with putting a little of this in.

However, if you are investing these valuable resources into an event then you should have a solid idea of what you want to get out at the other end. This is the first step to a successful event—you must know what you want to achieve with the event. This might be to make new connections, grow your network, or to look for new people for the next coliving space. But these objectives are not enough on their own. They might be a good starting point (an overarching idea), but there needs to be a lot more flesh on the bone if this is going to work. Think SMART objectives to really put you in the right frame of mind when it comes to this. This stands for Specific, Measurable, Achievable, Realistic and Time-bound. Knowing what you really want will help the rest of the planning.

For example, you don't just want to say that you will grow your network. You should state that you want to grow your network by getting the specific contact details of ten new people and following these up with a phone call or message within 7 days of the event finishing with the aim of adding them to a mailing list about new coliving opportunities in your area. You get the gist? This is about far more than having a good time—but rest assured, a good time will follow.

From this simple idea about an achievable goal, you can plan the rest of the event. The end goal will determine the number of people you invite, the kind of event it is and the entertainment you will put on. For instance, if you want to attract at least ten new people, then a small gathering for a meal where you invite five people will never achieve the aim you have set out. Think long and hard about how these things fit together. Over time you will be able to develop this into a task that you will know instinctively. You may work out that 50% of the people you invite attend, and then 25% of the attendees actually want to give their details, as an example. Working back from the target figure of ten in this example, you will need to invite 80 people to get the ten new names you want. It is about thinking of your coliving business in this way that helps you treat it like an actual business—one that will help others while making you some cash at the same time.

The numbers are only a small part of the planning. You might want your next coliving space to be one where artists, actors, writers and musicians hang out together. If this is the case then you will need to look in these communities and make the event specific to them. You might have a vacancy in an existing coliving space for a professional that works in the marketing world. Whatever it is you are aiming for, make sure that the event is geared up perfectly to make this happen. There is so much panning that needs to be done in order to make the event work as well as it should.

The Event Itself

On the day of the event, you need to get all of your ducks in a row. Rather than thinking about things last minute (when in all likelihood you'll want to be getting ready) it's best to set up as soon as you can. Delegation is a vital part of this. If you have a cook employed in the coliving space, then get them to take care of all the food. If it's a coliving space that already has people living there, then get them to help out and make the most of the event since it benefits them too. An hour or so of helping will be well worth the entertainment and free refreshments they'll be able to enjoy during the event!

As the host of an event, it's important that you are free to deal with any issues as well as mingle with the people that you invited. A large part of the event's success is that people feel the lifestyle, get excited by it, and want to become involved. To make this happen, you need to be as relaxed and on-the-ball as you possibly can. Doing the food or putting up decorations at the last minute will put you in a position where you might feel stressed or disconnected from people. That's the last thing you want. Some of this comes from the way you get organized before the event, but it's also about your mindset. Don't feel the need to do everything in this situation— spend time speaking to people with all the passion you have about coliving and what a difference it can make in the life of others.

The event should run as smoothly as possible. So, with this in mind, you might want to take on the expense of having an organizer do this on your behalf. A party planner or someone similar will get everything set up right on the day and deal with any issues as they go. All you need to do is explain exactly what you want and then pay them for their success at the end. Most will want some money up front as a retainer and then the remainder of their fee at the end. They may need you to grab the cash to pay suppliers too, but this is something you would already be doing if you were to take care of it yourself.

And this is the mindset you need to take into the event. If you free up your time to be yourself and achieve your objectives, then you are in the best position to make it a success. That will make all the difference!

Post-Event

All of this is great, but the success is really in the follow up. If you achieve the objective of connecting with a heap of people and then never do anything with these relationships, then you are wasting valuable time and money with the event. There are only so many times you can do this and waste your hard-earned cash. So definitely get in touch with these people, follow up quickly, and actually use the event to its fullest to widen your network.

Connections are only useful if they are one or more of the following things:

- Active

  -You must be in touch with them on a regular basis
- Relevant

  -They should be in the market for what you are offering
- Local

  -If you are setting up a coliving space in LA, for instance, then connections in Paraguay don't really apply
- Valued

  -People want to work with people like themselves

So, after the event, you need to cement these connections and make sure you get the most from your event. Without a follow up, these people are just like those you met at a party once, they are individuals that you have encountered but not added to your network. All of the elements in this book that come together to make a successful coliving business are much easier if you have a wider network: recruitment, advertising, filling vacancies, marketing, and every other factor.

An event is the ideal way to widen that network and become a more connected person. But only if you do it correctly. Think about how you can make all of this work to your benefit. Planning before, freeing yourself up during, and following up after all sit in line with this ideal.

These events should be incredible. A simple gathering of a few people without a great deal of entertainment doesn't cut it here. You need an awesome event if it's going to attract people to what you do. Remember that for most people, coliving is a completely new concept. If you are going to showcase its best features, then you should make it as exciting and entertaining as possible. This means that you should think big—as BIG as you possibly can! Nobody reached the stars when aiming for the ground.

Your event will be the first of many. With this in mind, make notes about what you did and what went right or wrong. As time goes by and you have more of these, these notes will help you to continually improve. Getting better at what you do all the time is inevitable if you are organized and understand what actually works. I suggest that you keep notes on many areas of the coliving journey you go on. This can end up being a nice thing to look back on or can be developed into a blueprint for future success, either for you or for others to follow.

Twelve

Technology

The technical amenities of coliving are another key attribute that sets it apart from all other traditional living methods. With residents having access to these valuable assets in their own home, the propensity for growth is amplified as one's ability to communicate and manage all parts of their life and business are streamlined. In addition, the higher density of residents in a coliving space than normal means that attention to technology is not just an asset but also a necessity in order to keep track of who is using certain resources at a time, as well as allocating an even distribution of these amenities.

Your home can often benefit from investing in valuable tech options to suit the particular needs of the tribe's work. These can not only enhance the shared connection between housemates and foster communal productivity, but also help them to work more effectively with the help of these resources. As costly as these amenities may seem for one person to shoulder, they can be realistically implemented across multiple residents. These will, of course, be specific to the preferences of your group. For example, the tribe may opt for a smart lock system to grant access to visitors if they interact frequently with guests or want to keep track of who is entering the property without needing to be physically present. Many of the people who go for coliving will be younger such as Millennials, or Gen Z, so things like good WiFi access are an absolute must. Accessing other technologies all start with excellent online access.

Technology for the sake of it helps nobody. There are over a million Apps available on the Apple App store alone, so you can see that embracing all technology isn't practical. What you need to do is identify the ones that will make the biggest difference in your coliving space. There will be certain things that you can't do without. Other pieces of technology just won't float your boat. This depends on the people you are living with and the way they want to use the coliving space. For some, this will be a place to work as well as rest and play. For others it will be purely a place to rest their head at the end of the day. Think about the characters in your coliving group and their needs to determine what will actually work best for the people in and around you.

Smart Home

Nobody wants to pay more than necessary on utilities. By using modern technology to personalize the level of control that housemates have over things like lighting and temperature, residents can maximize comfort while keeping costs down. A lot of options on the market can be controlled by phone or programmed to turn off at certain times when spaces aren't occupied. This reasonable approach to power consumption allows members to contribute to the common goal of reducing unnecessary expenses that they all are responsible for. Check out all of the different options available and set up those that work best for your living space. Leaving the air conditioning unit on when you're out for the whole day may give you a nice cold room to return to, but it'll cost a large amount of cash in the meantime. Accessing the electrical devices in the home remotely will allow all the occupants to keep down the costs for themselves and each other. Look for Apps in this area that work on a range of smartphone and tablet devices so that all housemates can use them on the move.

Home hubs have really taken hold over the last couple of years, so a device like the Amazon Echo can change the way you all live. They link to their parent company so you can put items in your shopping basket, change radio stations, or leave reminders for yourself or others in the home. These are relatively inexpensive and can help coordinate other items in the smart home too, so you have a central point of reference.

Smart appliances are becoming more widespread and can really help cut out waste and make living in the home a much more enjoyable experience. From the smart refrigerator that lets you know if there are items of food in your fridge going bad to the smart vacuum that scans the floor while you get on with your day, there are always items to make the coliving space more pleasurable and easier to maintain. The beauty of a coliving tribe is that you can spread the cost of these items across the number of people living there. Some may feel like they are expensive purchases for one person, but divided by the people in your unit, they can become inexpensive quite quickly.

You can also find devices that help you cook items, bake, and barbecue at top quality. The last thing you want is poorly cooked food (especially if you decide not to hire a chef) or cookware that's damaged and needs replacing. Think about the solutions you can get out there that will keep you all safe from having to go out and buy new cookware because the previous ones are damaged or broken due to mishandling or burned food.

Technology is best used when it's easy to operate and adds to the way you live. All of the above have the ability to do that but be aware that not all of these will apply to your living space. Coliving is about getting the best results and listening to each other. Maybe a meeting once per month or quarterly can help you to all put forward ideas on what your coliving technology use looks like and whether anything needs to be changed. Having an automated life will help you to get the most from coliving. It's one of the biggest benefits. So there should always be time to double check and make sure it still serves this purpose.

Apps

There are endless Apps available to make life easier and many of them can be used by coliving homes to deliver better results. And that's what we are all about! If there is an App available that takes some strain off and gives you an easier life, then we say go for it. Here are some of the highlights that will bring you all something a little better.

IFTTT

Known as 'If This Then That.' This is a handy little App that works on the principle of one thing prompting another. For instance, want the lights to come on if you get within half a mile of your home? If so then program IFTTT to do this. It will geo-locate your phone and then click on the lights via your smart device. Want the work phone to go straight to voicemail during the weekend? IFTTT can do this for you too. All you need to do is set the wheel in motion on the App and let it do all the hard work for you. There are a host of preset ideas on there, or you can come up with your own if they don't suit your circumstances. This means that you can arrange your home around your life and not the other way around. Setting them to act in the way we want or expect takes a lot of the strain away and puts you firmly in control.

Private FB Secret Group

It's a good idea to set up a Facebook group for your coliving space so that people can receive necessary updates and correspond with one another. We have one for Kindred Quarters. Since the content will be fairly specific and personal in nature, this page should ideally be made private. In this group, prospective housemates can enter as well as past ones who have since moved on, allowing for productive conversations about experiences and expectations to ensure transparency and satisfaction for everyone involved. The best way for everyone to get the most from the living space you occupy is to be open and share their experiences, good or bad. Rather than steep this in negativity, you can all use this information to make your life better.

If you have the right people in the first place, then you will have positive information to pass between you and make the very most of the place you live in. Imagine sharing the best ways to stay cool in the summer in a particular room or those hard-to-find places to eat around the neighborhood. This is the perfect way to make the most of a private Facebook group for all involved. For Kindred Quarters, we actually have a secret group with everyone that's ever stayed at one our homes. Whether that be as a guest for one night or a longtime resident, we like to stay in touch. Since because we've built such a tight community, we can communicate with each other in there.

Airbnb

Your space might decide to use Airbnb in order to make the most of the opportunities this website offers. Airbnb is a great way to fill some of the spaces you have in the property on an irregular basis. If you want to maximize income by renting out your room every now and again, then this is the website that will work hand-in-hand with your goals. Simply register with Airbnb and upload all the relevant details about the coliving space you occupy. Obviously, you'll need to get the permission of everyone living there, so they aren't surprised to find random strangers in the bathroom one morning. You can set the times where any part of the living space is available. Working together on this one can really help bring in some additional income (you or one of your housemates might spend a lot of time away with work or traveling) and keeps the place feeling vibrant and fresh with new energy. With the cost of living so high, bringing in that extra money will help you to keep control of costs.

Google Calendar

Use Google calendar as a simple way to let others in the house know what's going on, whether it's in terms of use or group events. Although Trello may be better for detailed tasks, the calendar is best for broader plans and transitioning them easily across other devices.

If your home opts for a rotational plan for certain amenities, rooms, or the laundry schedule, these can also be tracked consistently on this platform. Google has a whole host of functions that are not always obvious at first. Using their calendars syncs your life with your smartphone (especially if you get the amazing Google G-Suite App), so you can see what's going on with your living space wherever you are in the world.

Being organized is an essential part of coliving and one that can be easily overlooked. Don't think that things will always sort themselves out and just fall into place. As I'm sure you already know from other areas of your life, this is rarely the case. You need to put something in to get what you want out of it at the other end. Being an organized group of people will help you all feel like this is working for you. It's simple to drop in to Google Calendar whenever you want and use the features to set reminders and prompts for all concerned. Having a party in a couple days' time? Just set a reminder the day before, the morning of, and about an hour before the party so that everyone keeps up. They may want to be a part of it or head out. Whatever their decision, Google Calendar will help you remember.

Trello

In a coliving space, collaboration is the name of the game. For this reason, Trello is a valuable tool to integrate into the project management duties of a coliving space. This assists in the streamlining of workflow to maximize efficiency. With the need to share meeting spaces and resources as well as communicate progress, the best way to organize tasks is by leaving nothing to the imagination.

You can use Trello to lay out duties for completion, detailing the time, duration, and details of each activity. Essentially, Trello can be utilized to separate tasks categorically, however you like. This gives users the ability to interactively conceptualize what's actually getting done.

Visualization is extremely important for productivity, and Trello presents content in the most digestible (and generally intuitive) manner possible for maximum results. Since individuals work in different ways and choose to arrange their tasks in whichever manner best suits them, the flexibility that Trello offers is uniquely appealing.

It can also be used to keep track of what others are doing in order to best strategize your own plans. This can be operated at any scale of preference, from each day to a full calendar overview. The ability to vote, comment, and include attached links in tasks ensures that users have access to as much information as desired about a given topic and are therefore best positioned to complete it. Although Trello does offer a vast array of options and customization, it's also pretty simple. This is important when dealing with various users and collaborators on the same platform. On top of all this, Trello is free. There's no need to invest in costly project management software when this one can serve you perfectly.

Cameras

Cameras can be a tool for safety as well as efficiency. In terms of security, the frequently larger size of coliving spaces means that it's not always easy to keep track of each nook and cranny at once. The use of cameras provides some peace of mind for residents to know what's going on surrounding the premises, and it also acts as a theft or trespassing deterrent. Since coliving involves more people in the home who are bound to have visitors for work or play, the installation of a doorbell camera creates ease of entry for incoming guests who can be buzzed in through a simple phone App. Think about how safe you want everyone in the living space to feel. Cameras are about increasing this feeling of security. If there's ever a dispute, then simply checking the images from the cameras will settle it quickly and effectively. The presence of these cameras will more than likely stop this from happening in the first place. Just don't forget to let new occupants know that there are cameras present and have them sign something.

If desired, you can even have cameras inside your home and have all your residents sign agreements that they know there's a camera in some of the common areas. Obviously this would be for communal spaces, not the showers or bedrooms. This might be in your ballpark if your coliving home involves a large number of guests or clients and visitors who frequently come in and out.

Cameras can be purchased and installed pretty inexpensively to meet this end. If you want something that offers great images that can also be recorded and played back with clarity, then you'll likely have to pay a little more if it's worth it to you. Look at any data protection laws applicable in your jurisdiction, but with this in mind you can provide a degree of security and comfort for all involved. Your concierge could be the person who has access to the images in the first instance and be the in the case of any disputes. You can also view your camera feed in real-time on a phone App. This should keep things on the straight and narrow and put away accusations of bias. It's great to have a level of security and protection for everyone in the coliving space, so think about cameras and how they can provide this in the best way.

Thirteen

Future Growth

In this section, we are going to cover the best course of action if you want to launch more locations. Companies like WiFi Tribe or Remote Year are more like travel-based businesses, but what's really cool is that they structure this around the world, digital nomad type of adventure. This is something that can be offered to current residents or to your list of followers, where they agree to pay a certain amount to come on a group trip and jump around the world while working remotely.

Hosting high-end events in Masterminds is just another way you can generate future revenue for your home. Also, consider hosting a one-day event, which I've done in the past, like a business intensive mastermind where your roommates come together and you charge admission for people to attend the event but they walk away with some amazing life or business strategies. There are so many fun and lucrative directions you can go in.

In order to open additional locations, whether they're within the same city or even a different country, you first have to make sure that your first house is completely dialed in with systems and automation. There's no need to expand to more locations if your first isn't fully in order. It can be exciting to build this concept further once you get a taste of it, but try not to get too eager or impatient. I am always a fan of trying to open up homes close to each other, since you can share resources between them like your housecleaner, chef, and personal assistant. You can also do joint events between the homes to expand your network even more!

The most important thing to do is start building an interest list or waiting list for your next house. This is the number one way to gauge when to actually open that next location. You need to make sure the demand is there so there's no loss of time and money if you're left with another home but nobody to live in it. Once you have that client base of expectant residents, then all you need to do is duplicate how you started the first home. If necessary, you can make any tweaks to the systems if you found that certain approaches worked a bit better in your first home after trial and error. This second go-around should be much better! That's another amazing thing about this process—it gets more intuitive and exciting each time you expand out.

Fourteen

Interviews & Case Studies

We wanted to dedicate a chapter to other perspectives on this new industry of coliving. You'll read firsthand accounts and experiences shared from current residents of Kindred Quarters, previous residents, and the best part is that we're also including interviews with some of the pioneer leaders of this new industry, owners of coliving homes around the world. We also included some special interviews with actual digital nomads to get some insight on the type of person who enjoys coliving and traveling the world and their personal motivation behind it.

With all of these authentic viewpoints, you can really get a feel for how it is living like this and the broad variety of ways in which it can be practiced. Enjoy!

All of these interview videos are also live on our YouTube channel (Kindred Quarters & The Coliving Code) where you can refer back to them as well as take in the full content since these were so long and packed with info that we had to shave it down a bit.

Debra Máres | Founder of Women Wonder Writers | KQ San Diego, Los Angeles

As startup founders, we're constantly flying; but the successful ones know where to land. For me, that's been at the Kindred Quarters Entrepreneur House. Colife has been a critical part of my personal and nonprofit organizational resilience this past year. If you're reading this book, my guess is you also are constantly pivoting, trying new ideas, rapidly scaling, flying through funnels, going from meeting-to-meeting, facing highs and lows in short spans of time, and managing staff.

What helps give a tranquility to this turbulence is having a safe harbor to not only rest your head, but colive with a tribe of mentors who support your great ideas and tell you when to give up the bad ones—including in dating! Colife gives me and my business hope to thrive, not simply survive. As peers, we can be vulnerable because we're experiencing similar struggles, we have access to each other's idea muscles during weekly masterminds, and we're all positive. This "co-intimacy" at home helps refuel us to get back in the air and fly around the next day, or even catch a tailwind.

One day, over a casual conversation in our kitchen, I expressed frustration about building company culture in my education nonprofit. KQ resident Josh Isaak of Breakthrough Physical Therapy Marketing looked at me and asked one simple question, "So how are you going to approach it?" The truth was I didn't know how to. Our staff worked remotely around Southern California and were mostly in the field mentoring youth. "We're not in an office together," I explained. Josh had a simple solution: "Town Hall Meeting." Josh walked me through the concept and shared how it worked for his company. Since that day, I've held Town Halls weekly via Zoom so our entire staff can attend and it's been game changing. The way that idea organically unfolded in the KQ kitchen is just one of many examples of coliving with benefits!

I first learned about coliving when I met KQ Founder and Author Chrissy in Bali, Indonesia while rooming together during a service retreat. Have you ever experienced that feeling when you meet someone and when you begin to observe them, see that something is really unique about them? That's what happened with Chrissy. I quickly noticed how well she had her travel life hacked. She had a very simple way of living, from forfeiting late nights to rising early, to keeping her hotel room space tidy and respecting mine, to meeting with other coliving experts in Bali while others were out shopping. I wanted to learn more about her entrepreneurial life and how coliving could support my goals.

I quickly borrowed Kindred Quarters' "profit and loss" mentality and concluded that if I can think less about meal prep, utility bills, rent, laundry, dry-cleaning, social life and who I'm going to bounce my next big idea off, I can be more present to build a resilient organization. And that will benefit the girls faced with trauma that we mentor at Women Wonder Writers. It's a win–win. Exactly a month from that trip, I began coliving in Los Angeles.

Additionally, being part of the coliving/coworking world has opened my eyes to a new business opportunity and gave me the confidence to start my own coliving home. I've begun searching for a home close to a college in the Inland Empire with the goal of providing graduate students the opportunity to colive and cowork. Giving the next generation of leaders a safe harbor so they can fly high like us at KQ is possible because of visionaries like Chrissy and practical tools she sets out in The Coliving Code.

That is what KQ is about. Together we can hack our lives to make the world a better place!

L-R: Debra Máres, WWW Founder and Author; Holden Sherbakov, The Greatness Foundation Ambassador, Bali Family; Chrissy McDaniel, The Coliving Code Author and KQ Founder participating in a puppet show following Debra's reading of It's This Monkey's Business children's book tackling domestic violence and divorce in Bali, Indonesia.

Dan Schwartz | CEO: InvestorFuse | KQ Alumni, San Diego

Hey. How's it going? This is Dan Schwartz and I lived at a Kindred Quarters house for six months in 2018. It was some of the most dialed in six months that I have ever had in my whole life, and I'll tell you why, and why I'd recommend you consider living in a coliving house just like Kindred Quarters.

Not only are the Kindred Quarters systems so dialed in that you don't really have to worry about too much of the day to day decision making, it also has a lot of other benefits that help your state of mind, help your health, and then help your relationships.

State of mind: the simplest way to explain this is less decisions equals less stress and anxiety, equals more productivity and mental energy to get stuff done through the day.

Having a private chef, having a concierge that makes your bed and takes care of any odds and ends that you need done really frees up a lot of mental bandwidth for you to accomplish at a much higher level. It's great for entrepreneurs that really need to focus and hone in on the 80/20 of their business.

Health wise, obviously having a private paleo chef is going to increase your health and vitality. Not having to worry about cooking is not only a huge time saver, but when you only have healthy food around, you create the environment for a healthy lifestyle. I can't recommend that enough. Just having the system dialed in.

Kindred Quarters is designed for an optimal lifestyle, and the best part of it is it's a social experience. You get to surround yourself with amazing like-minded, growth-driven people that are all working on different areas, different industries of business that you can learn from and pull some knowledge into your business. Not only do you have the accountability, but you have the events. We had events all the time. This is one of the great things about Kindred Quarters is the community that it helps build. When you're at the center of the community, it gives you so many opportunities to meet so many new people.

For me, I'm sort of introverted, so I like to do stuff on my own and really retreat inwards from my own thoughts in figuring out big decision in business, in life. But when I'm living in a coliving environment, I'm forced into the social situations that actually help me grow as a person.

If that sounds like something you're interested in, I highly recommend coliving as an option for housing & community. I wish you the best of luck. Thanks. Peace.

Austin Netzley | CEO & Founder of 2X | KQ Los Angeles Current Resident

Hey, this is Austin Netzley. I'm the founder of 2X and I wanna give a quick shoutout to Chrissy and the entire Kindred Quarters team and talk quickly about my experience with Kindred Quarters. So I've known Chrissy for a couple of years now; this is actually the second house that I've lived in. I'm in the LA house, I lived in the San Diego house originally and just couldn't give a higher praise about the experience, about Chrissy. It gets smoother and better every single time but imagine just being able to work on your business and have some fun and rest and everything else be handled. Imagine what that's like, imagine having amazing events and be surrounded with awesome people and have that built in networking community and tribe all around you. And just have everything so dialed in. Well that's what's possible, that's what Chrissy's created here with Kindred Quarters and I couldn't say that's it's been... it couldn't have possibly be an easier and better experience, seriously.

I've known Chrissy since the first entrepreneur house that I lived in and things have just been so dialed in since then. Amazing chef, amazing amenities such as a really, really high speed internet and amazing people around us. We have an event tonight, we have another event Saturday night. Like it's amazing stuff going on and I don't have to do anything. It's awesome. I can work on my business, play, and sleep. Like that's pretty much it and everything else is taken care of, so it takes out a lot of decisions that you need to make or most people need to make throughout the day and is just an awesome, awesome experience all around. You connect with amazing people, find your tribe, have more success than ever, have your life just dialed in so you can do more of what you really wanna do.

That's it from my standpoint, the main significance and value of Kindred Quarters and the coliving communities. And I could not recommend Chrissy and the Kindred Quarters team enough. So contact her and get lined up for one of the many and awesome houses that are coming out. Be a part of this tribe, be a part of this community, and you'll forever be a part of the family.

Interview with Haz Memon | Founder of Swiss Escape in Switzerland

Haz has two homes that he's running in Switzerland which he started two years ago. We talk about a lot of things, including how he got started and also where he sees the industry of coliving going in the future. He's actually spoken on different industry panels for coliving, which is exciting. He comes to us today through the powers of the internet. He's actually in Budapest, Hungary for the month doing some coworking and coliving over there. So let's go ahead and get right into it. Again, I'm super excited to bring these interviews to you guys. I'm doing one each week with different founders.

Christine: Okay, so I am here with Haz. He's the cofounder of Swiss Escape. I'm super excited to interview him first on this series. I'm just reaching out to different founders of coliving spaces, since finally this industry is starting to take off. They have some amazing knowledge. I'm going to go ahead and launch right into it. Haz, do, you mind telling us more about the Swiss Escape?

Haz: Yeah, so thank you for having me. It's really important that we get this word out. I'm really passionate about coliving movement in itself. So, Swiss Escape started two years ago. It is in the French speaking part of the Swiss Alps. So, very focused towards nature, and towards bringing entrepreneurs together and such alike in one space so we can create some signature.

Christine: Love it. Then you started it how long ago?

Haz: Two years ago. It was two years ago and it all actually started in Lisbon because I was in the regular 9 to 5 as we were all in that kind of work flow. But I was always into tourism. I always loved traveling. I was like, how can I make sure that I'm always traveling, but always meeting inspiring people? My journey started in Lisbon where I went to really network with entrepreneurs and get ideas on what do entrepreneurs really want, and what they are missing. That's where I found the idea of coliving and how this is growing in the whole millennial age. So, we came back and we're like, hey, there's nothing happening in Switzerland of this kind. Switzerland in itself is very big on technology and housing and things like that. A lot of the housing was quite expensive. If you think about just buying a house, or even renting one yourself. So, we were like, why don't we convert a beautiful shelly in the Alps into a coliving space and just test it out. Just right after the first week launch, we started getting bookings. We had quite a few interests. Then we saw more and more people getting into it. I think right after the first year, we immediately got the second property. So we are now on two properties.

Christine: Nice. And then how many people can stay in each property?

Haz: In each property there eight people, we can fit eight people. Together, up to 15 to 16 people.

Christine: Okay, and they each have a private room, or does anybody share an actual room?

Haz: People can choose. Because we've designed our space in a way that we have modular beds so that it can be switched into a single room or a shared bedroom. We move according to what the demand is.

Christine: Oh, nice. Then when you guys got the second house, were there any changes that you guys said, okay, let's do things a little differently. Obviously it's trial and error with a first house. So what things did you change when you guys got the second one?

Haz: Yeah. What was great was the owner of the space itself was also the owner of the second space. So, it was really easy to negotiate in that sense. We really wanted it unfurnished this time so we could choose what we wanted to put, and how we wanted to design the space. Designing the space was very important because after the first year of experience we saw that how people move around and how behavior changes across the rooms. We installed some things which are very different from the first space like we've got a garage which has a ski storage system. Initially, we had to rent out ski lockers. But now, we have within the space as ski storage, and we've got boot warmers and a lot of the storage space I think was very important.

Then also we realized the kitchen in itself had to be more accessible for everyone to use at the same time, because sometimes it was like some people were using it, and then others could not. We had to make sure that we are able to manage that. Then of course overall speaking of coliving spaces we had to implement some sort of guides and rules within the house to mitigate the whole environment.

Christine: Can you give me one or two of your guys' rules for the house? What were the things you've noticed that needed that implemented? Because we have resident commitments, we have seven different things that they commit to and it's general stuff to make the house run as smooth as possible. What were some of yours?

Haz: I think for us, it's mainly because we have a coworking space within the house, right? Then we have a Skype room, a dedicated Skype room. We wanted to make sure that others are not being disturbed when people are on calls. We had to make a rule that hey, if you have calls, we've got a dedicated room for that, and you should use that instead of doing it in the common coworking space. So, do not disturb others. That's one of the house rules that we created. Second being, it's just very simple but we had a board where everyone can put up ideas on what they want to learn, and what they want to teach. That was very good for us to also implement events, then, okay, someone wants to go skiing this weekend or someone wants to do that, that we have a place where everything can be put.

Christine: That's a great idea. How often do you guys have events?

Haz: Every week. I would say twice a week at least. There's always one business event and one social event. Every week.

Christine: That's awesome. Is it just within the homes or do you guys invite outside people?

Haz: We are in a small town, so we don't have a lot of people who are into this entrepreneurial life. More and more we organize events in big cities so we can bring more people. But usually, it's just an in-house event.

Christine: Awesome. We should have started with this, but tell people where you're from and then where you're currently living. Definitely a digital nomad. You can run anything remotely.

Haz: Yeah. That was the whole idea of it, right? If I'm running a business which could cater to the digital nomad, then I need to experience what it is like to be a digital nomad, right? So, I'm originally from Dubai, and I moved to Switzerland about six years ago. From then on, I've been working in the travel industry. I've moved around, I've lived in Netherlands for a while as well. It's really now that we've got this coliving space up and growing that it allows me to move around a bit more, and really push this coliving movement like Christine you said it. I often try to get involved in conferences or give talks at coworking spaces about future work and about how coliving is playing a crucial role in that. I'm in Budapest, and it's just a lovely place to be.

Christine: That's great because you practice what you preach. You're a cofounder. Is there one other person?

Haz: Yes. My cofounder is actually my partner, my girlfriend, basically. So, it was very interesting to start a business with your own partner. At first, it's a little different than starting with someone you don't know. But for us, it worked really well, because we already knew how we work, and we set rules right at the beginning and roles and responsibilities. I think it just works.

Christine: Nice, that's great. What are your favorite parts about running a coliving home?

Haz: I think the first and foremost is just meeting inspiring people every day. I think that just makes me want to do it more and more. I think that's one of my favorite part for sure. Second, is also how I understand different cultures. Because initially, when we launched, the first booking we had was a girl from Singapore. Then we had bookings from Norway, to US, to Brazil. When you bring all these people in one house, it's just an amazing experience. Then I learned so much about these countries, and I'm like, "Hey, I want to go there too. Because I've never thought this would be so exciting." Yeah, definitely.

Christine: Oh, that's great. Same thing. My number one by far is just that you're learning about different cultures and then having these different, amazing, inspiring people live with you. You see how they live, you become close friends, and then it's sad though when they leave, right? But then when I travel to their country, we hang out. I'm on the other side of the world in Paris, I got to hang out with somebody who had lived with us last summer, because that's where he's from. By chance, we were there at the same time. So I agree 110% it's just meeting new people, building new relationships, and then learning about new cultures.

Haz: I think it's a really a small world because almost every place I've traveled, I've found someone I already knew before. Either directly or either because someone told me, "Hey, my friends is there, just go and catch up and have a coffee or a drink. Great." I don't need to even look for people, I've just got people everywhere now.

Christine: Even in Bali, the same thing, I bumped into a friend. He knew I was coming into town. I was going to meet with him that weekend, but I was there at the cafe to meet with somebody else and then he just happened to be there and then we bumped into each other. How do I bump into somebody on the other side of the world? I think you're right, the world is just becoming more connected and smaller. That's always a good thing. Oh, so I want to know, and I'm sure the people watching too, what's the average stay? Do you offer nightly, weekly, monthly? And then what's the average age?

Haz: Also worth mentioning, I think most of the people that we attract are entrepreneurs, and some of them are remote workers and freelancers, but most are entrepreneurs. They have their own businesses and they are able to run it remotely. Given that they are actually quite young, I would say somewhere around the age of 23 to 40. Guys and girls. I think there's no specific preference. I think it's everyone who is into nature and sports. We have an average stay of about three weeks in the winter season, and about two weeks in the summer season. Usually, because winter season for us is very much focused on skiing and snowboarding and things like that, so people like to stay longer because they usually get a season pass and they want to hang out for a month or two months at least. Whereas in summers, they want to go for hikes or paraglide or things like that. It's very exciting that we get to see two different kinds of people, and enthusiasts because we're like winter sports and summer sports. So, it's two kinds of people.

Christine: Is there a minimum stay? Could somebody save for a night, or do you have a minimum?

Haz: The minimum has to be for a week.

Christine: Then what's your occupancy usually run? Are you fully occupied 100% of the time?

Haz: In our winter season, I would say we are occupied 90% of the time. Also, winter season is something we get booked quite early. Because sometimes we get bookings a year in advance. Winter season is quite full in that sense. Whereas in summer season, our occupancy is a bit lower, I would say about 50% or 60%. But we try to push that more to events that we're organizing.

Christine: Oh, perfect. Do you keep in touch with people that have stayed there? Do you build a relationship with all of them, keep in touch with them?

Haz: Yeah. Like you said, they end up being friends. We're always in touch. Last week, there was a person who stayed with us in Swiss Escape in January, and he was in Budapest last weekend. He just wrote to me, "Hey, you want to catch out for a drink? I'm in Budapest." I'm like, "Great, let's do that." We really connect on a personal level. And it's not just about how I am running the space, and you are the guest and I have this mirror between us. It's more like I'm completely transparent with everything I do and business wise is also personal in the personal sense. I really connect with them on a personal level. They're all my Facebook friends as well. So, I regularly chat with them on WhatsApp or on Facebook.

Christine: Then when you're in Switzerland, do you stay at your own property? Is that where you always stay?

Haz: The first year we were staying at their own property, but since the demand increased, now we've got a third property where it's just the cofounders staying.

Christine: Are you're going to expand that or is it a smaller place?

Haz: Right now it's a smaller place. It's just a two bedroom apartment where we are just the cofounders staying. But if we see more and more demand then we can, of course, expand to more spaces. But right now, we had to step out of the coliving spaces in order to give the availability for others to join in.

Christine: Well, that's a good problem to have, right? It's funny. The LA house got overbooked, and I literally was on an air mattress, sharing one of the bedrooms with a good friend of mine. Again, it's a good problem to have, but the next month, a lot of our housemates are traveling for summertime. They'll be gone for a week or two weeks. So, now we put their rooms on Airbnb to get those filled just for the short term. Again, good problems to have, but I'm just trying to figure out the delicate balance of availability and not letting a room sit vacant either.

Haz: I think for us, it's really about prioritizing people. Usually, when we have people who are coming back the second time or third time, they have a priority over new bookings. Also, the new bookings we always warn them that, "Hey, we have limited availability. So, if you want something you need to pre-book well in advance." I think people get their message quite clearly. That's why we get early bookings.

Christine: Do you give a discount to return bookers?

Haz: Yes, a 10% discount.

Christine: All right, perfect. Haz has amazing blog on Medium. So, I know you're super active in this industry. You speak at different conferences. What events do you usually attend?

Haz: Everything tech related. I've been to Web Summit, which is the biggest conference in Europe around the tech industry, which happens every year. So, I try to get to that as much as I can. I've also been to Nomad City where I've been a speaker. This was a panel of coliving space founders and coworking space founders talking about some of the challenges and some of the future that we see here. But at the same time, I also have done something completely different, which is a nomad cruise. I don't know if you guys have heard about that.

Christine: Oh, we've heard of that! What year did you do it?

Haz: I did last year, last fall, from Spain to Panama. It was amazing. It's basically a conference on a cruise ship. You have a two weeks long Atlantic cruise, and you've got conference every day. It's also learning at the same time, but you're also taking a bit of a detox from using your laptops and your phone all the time. You get really into the talks and the workshops there. I think this is really a place where I can meet people. That's why I try to do as much as possible to create some sort of an influence about the whole coliving movement.

Christine: And then that's my last question for you, is where do you see this industry going?

Haz: I really see this as a norm. I would see it just like hotels or Airbnb has become. I would see called living as just an option that every city has around the world. That you could either go into a hotel, either go into an Airbnb hostel, or a coliving space that you should be able to find anywhere and everywhere you go.

Christine: And, this might just be here in the States, but, we're struggling with homeowners and property management companies understanding the concept. They've been shying away with it. They don't like the word subleasing, they're very particular about who they want to rent their home to. Have you found that to be an issue at all yet in this industry?

Haz: I think it happens in quite a lot in cities where the demand is high. But I think the important part is to negotiate with the owner about, hey, if this is how much you make in a year, this is how much we promise to get you in a year. If we can guarantee them that they get their 100K or 200K in a year then they're happy with that.

Christine: So, the lease is just in your name there? Again, Switzerland might be completely different. Then they don't care who comes in and out. You just guarantee that rent for them.

Haz: Yes, exactly.

Christine: Okay, cool. Got it. I think you're right. I think in cities like LA, San Diego, it's such a housing shortage so they can afford to be a little more picky about who they're having. But same thing, if we guarantee the rents and sign a longer lease, that would be a plus. And that's the direction I want to go in, educating these property management companies and real estate people. So let's get there sooner than later.

Haz: Yeah, I think it's nice to always put on a bit of a presentation of what you think you want to do with the space, or what has been happening around the whole coliving movement with examples of something like China investing $11 billion in a coliving building. Once you put facts into perspective, I think they see it more clearly. I would hope so at least.

Christine: Exactly. Haz, what's the best way for people to find out more about what you're up to?

Haz: Yeah, definitely. We run quite a bit of events. I would definitely subscribe to the Swiss Escape newsletter on our website to get the latest updates. Also, if you want to reach out to me personally, I'm fully accessible via email or Facebook or anything.

Christine: Perfect. Of course, if you ever want to take a trip to Switzerland, you can stay there, the Swiss Escape. I know now, that's going to be on my travel list. But I appreciate you taking the time today to do this interview. Thank you so much.

Haz: Definitely appreciate it, Christine. I really enjoyed talking with you as well. I'm happy to be part of this. Thanks.

....

Website: swissescape.co

Interview with Jacob Shapiro | Outpost Coliving in New York

This was a long one but packed full of content, so we have the full video up on our YouTube channel if you want to catch the full thing, plus the awesome guided tour that Jacob gives of the home.

Christine: Okay, hey guys, I am here with Jacob Shapiro, super excited to have him on. He is actually in front of one of their locations. He is with Outpost and he is the New York Account Manager, right?

Jacob: Correct, yep.

Christine: But you've been there since the beginning, so you know the company inside and out, that's why we're very excited, because you guys have four partners, right? Four different people?

Jacob: Three plus me. And then yep, we manage basically our 14 part-time and full-time employees.

Christine: Give us a little bit of history of Outpost. And again, you guys are just strictly based on New York, right?

Jacob: So, as a brief history, Outpost was started by three guys who came to the United States and realized how unfortunate really the New York renting market is. It's a terrible process if you want to go through it. It's really high barrier financially to enter with first and last month's rent, plus a security deposit equivalent to a full month's rent. You could empty your entire bank account doing that. You need to have background checks and credit checks, which many international arrivals do not have. And many other financial barriers and simply you can be denied for no apparent reason. So they didn't like that and decided to recreate the process for housing in New York City to make it as easy, or at least this is our goal, to make it easy as buying a cup of coffee.

Christine: I love that, that's a great USP, that's awesome. And you guys have how many locations total and how many rooms total?

Jacob: We have eight locations spread out between Brooklyn and Queens at the moment and we have 160 beds.

Christine: And then it takes a team, like you said, you guys have a good team to manage it all. What's your current occupancy rate roughly?

Jacob: Depends on the time of year. So, as most coliving spaces go through seasonality, so do we. During the summer is our high season, we operate around 80 to 90% occupancy while kind of the rest of the year is more 60 to 70%.

Christine: You live in one of the concepts right now, have you lived in one of the homes the whole time?

Jacob: Yeah. Since I moved in, literally the first day I started working I moved in to our Flatbush House located in Flatbush, Brooklyn. I lived there for about a month and kind of became really good friends with the people who lived at that house. From there I moved to our Knickerbocker House and I stayed there again, for about three, four months and in the process of filling that house up I moved to our Ridgewood House, which is where I've been for the last year.

Christine: Nice. We were kind of kidding around a little but before this interview because sometimes the houses get overbooked, especially in high season. But you said you guys sometimes get all in one room because you start renting out all the available beds. You want to talk about that?

Jacob: Yep. Specifically in the beginning, the owners had the Flatbush House and then the Knickerbocker House, that's kind of the progression of the houses, and after the Flatbush House filled up, they had nowhere to go and they had to basically open a new house to house themselves as well as others. Which caused them to open the Knickerbocker House, and from there that house all moved in eventually all into one room so that they could rent all the other rooms, and then opened up the Ridgewood House.

Christine: #startuplife. We've all been there. Oh my gosh, that's awesome, Jacob. You've already kind of talked about the evolution of how each home has started, is the growth more rapid? Is it quicker now with the purchasing of the homes? On scale right now?

Jacob: Yeah. Well, to clarify, we'll start there, our homes are not purchased. We, at the moment, are renting our houses but plan to do two purchased houses once we get a round of funding. Yeah, so it depends on how you want to grow. If you would like to go the rental route you have less control of the house obviously, because you don't own it, but you do get to grow quicker because the amount of investment startup, the startup investment is a smaller amount. New York houses, you can imagine the prices. Yeah, that's basically the way it goes. If you decide to own the house you get a lot more freedom to do what you want with the house, but you also probably won't grow as fast unless you have some major source of capital.

Christine: No, and that was actually two of my questions because we're same exact thing in California. Your prices are higher, you guys beat us. That's what Kindred Quarters is doing, I'm self funded, we're not taking outside money quite yet. We've had the offers and I'm like, "The investors stop. The market is way too high right now. I wouldn't even purchase, let's wait until a correction."

Jacob: So you're waiting for, yeah. You're waiting for the price to go down. Same. Yeah, yeah, same. That's a good point.

Christine: So on the funding side, are you guys actively searching for funding right now, or no?

Jacob: We are. We are currently in the running for an accelerator program called NUMA. NUMA is an accelerator based here. Actually they're based in Paris, they have locations around the world. They're actually the oldest accelerator in the world. We've been speaking with many of their members to basically see if we'd be a right fit for their program. But if we decide to go with them that would probably be the next 10 months of our lives. Looking for funding and doing that.

Christine: And then you guys haven't gone private equity, approached any BCs?

Jacob: We have approached BCs individually, but generally, at least in New York, they like for people to go through accelerators, incubators to be contacted as those guys are vouching on your behalf. But our original round of funding was kind of a family and friends thing, small amount of money allowed us to open up. From there, we've opened up our houses.

Christine: Nice, that's exciting. Now, jumping back to lease term, how long of a lease do you guys sign on the properties?

Jacob: Depends on the property, but the longer the better. Generally it's around five. Five years.

Christine: Okay, because you guys are going in and furnishing these homes too, right?

Jacob: Correct, yep. Exactly.

Christine: Okay, cool. Because we did a three year in L.A. Yeah, three to five, I agree, three to five. I've heard of some coliving companies doing 10 year leases. That's a long time. I'd like to start buying before then. And then what does your typical day include? Because again, this is nice, I've been interviewing the software side of coliving, I've done interviews with the founders, so now it's nice to kind of meet in the trenches, every day, all day.

Jacob: Good question. So as I mentioned, my title is New York Account Manager, which is intentionally vague simply because you know just as well as I do, startups, everyone's doing everything, right? In my typical day, to break it down very simply, I do three main things. First I do business to business sales, so if I contact New York based businesses, it seems as if their members, or students, or business partners will need short term or temporary housing, more like midterm housing, we only rent for longer than a month. If they need that we will contact them and set up business accounts with them. So that's my main sales aspect is I deal with the business to business sales. Second piece on the operational side is I do cross-departmental operations. So if the sales team needs to talk to our house leaders, if our house leaders need to talk to our handyman or our operations team, I facilitate those types of conversations to make sure more project based things get done. Lastly, I would say is just formalizing processes that haven't been created yet. So, anything from creating the operations manual, to originally when we created the sale process I was part of creating the original sales process of how potential clients become current clients become alumni. And really everything in between, how to hold events, how to get funding for events, our members can hold events as well, our house leaders hold events as well. Creating that process, formalizing everyone's job description, I've done all that.

Christine: What is the demographic actually of the people that stay at the home? And you said it's a one month minimum, you guys don't do less than a month, right?

Jacob: Correct, yep. That's just based off New York housing policy. We operate within the law of New York City. So, our demographic is basically about half American, half international. About 30% students and the rest are people who are already in their profession, and when I say students it's really of every background, right? Undergrad, graduate, and doctorate, it's all the same. And what else, age group is probably between 20 and 35, but we've hosted many people who are older than 35. And yeah.

Christine: That's great. It seems like this demographic too is more trusting, they leave their stuff out, we leave laptops out, iPhones, all sorts of stuff laying out.

Jacob: Right. So true.

Christine: We don't lock the doors half the time. You guys, same thing in your guys' neighborhood? In your homes?

Jacob: Exactly. Yeah, even being in New York City we're okay with that. Our outdoor, that door behind me, obviously has a lock on it. The door to the physical apartment obviously has a lock on it, however in the house there are no locks on doors to bedrooms. That's one, because of fire code, we're not allowed to do that. But two, because we're trying to create a communal atmosphere and the design decisions that you make within the home make nonverbal communications or nonverbal points of reference for your members, right? If you have locks on doors it's basically saying, "Keep your stuff in your room. Don't move your stuff out of your room." Even if we were allowed to do it, we wouldn't have done it. We also have other ways to keep people safe as well. There are lockers throughout the house if you do want to use your valuables, but if we were to go inside right now, there are no lockers. No one is using the lockers, that is to say. There are no locked valuables.

Christine: Oh my God, I love that concept. No, that's amazing and I think you're exactly right that you're going to deter the people that are super fearful and that energy of them being scared someone's going to steal their stuff, scared of, you know. You're going to deter those people if you're like, "Hey, this is how we live. We don't lock these doors. Your stuff's fine." I think you're going to have more of those carefree people that aren't super attached to physical belongings and it creates a better energy. Let's see here, do you guys have a list of house rules or guest commitments, roommate, any sort of set of rules that you guys give people when they live in?

Jacob: Absolutely, yep. People sign a membership agreement, which is basically a lease. It's very extensive, more extensive than your average lease simply because of the amenities that are included in the house. So yes, we do have rules and then there are little rules around the house to explain basically how you should interact with aspects of the house. One of our lovely house leaders is a graphic designer and he had designed for us three sets of rules that we get to put all around the house. Actually, four sets of rules. So there's one for the kitchen, one for the whole house, one for the bedrooms, and then little signs that go around that are non-English signs. They're all signage, like icons. So that people of any language capability can understand how to interact with those things.

Christine: Yeah, because you already said 50% of your guys' occupants are international. Wow, okay, cool.

Jacob: A lot of them, not a lot of them, but I'd say 80 to 90% have full English-speaking capabilities, but many of them are here for a language school. So they are learning English. So there's a decent portion of them that are doing that as well.

Christine: Do you do events at your homes?

Jacob: We do. Each house has two events per month, and anyone from any house can go to any event. So, basically people have access to around two events per week.

Christine: Okay, cool. Do you guys invite outside people to those events also?

Jacob: We do. All the events can be found in the back end of our website. Once you become a current member you can RSVP yourself and your friends. Friends are paid though, right? Member are paying for these events and a friend is not paying for access to the event, so we charge for them. Depends on the event. If it doesn't cost us any money, it doesn't cost them any money. But, yeah.

Christine: Definitely. Again, coliving is such a new industry, so it's exciting that you've been in it for a couple of years already. So what's your personal opinion on the future of coliving?

Jacob: I would say we haven't seen every iteration of the niche yet, right? We're a niche category in real estate, right? But within that niche there will be other smaller niches, right? You mentioned before it would be really cool to open houses for single mothers, it would be really cool to open houses as there already are for entrepreneurs, it would be really cool to open houses for artists, as there again, already is. We haven't seen all those and I don't know, other than the entrepreneurial bout, the viability financially for some of those things. I like it, I love the idea, sounds super cool, but I heard this other real estate investor talk about location and that location is your best and your worst asset, right? Because if you have a great location, that's great, but you also can never move your location, right? Sometimes single mother house sounds fantastic for single mothers to live in, but it's just not the right neighborhood, right? This guy, he said, "Money talks, but real estate does not walk." You know? So, it's a great way of saying it. While location can be a great asset, it can also limit the scope of people capable of living in your house. For us, we are intentionally non-interspaced based, right? We have some houses that form their own small interspace groups, but people move in and out, so those waves come and go, right? Yeah, I'd say for the future it looks bright. As I mentioned in the beginning, looking to create a new type of real estate product that is as easy as buying a cup of coffee, as I mentioned. I can go a little bit further into that so you kind of understand what I mean by that. If you go to Starbucks, you know how much a cup of coffee costs, before even walking in. You know around how much it costs. You know how much the upgrade should cost. You know that a latte is going to be more expensive than a cup of coffee. You know that if you go to a Starbucks anywhere in the world it's going to be a similar cost and the same cup of coffee. And you know that international brand is safe and it can be found basically anywhere if you open your phone. None of those consumer luxuries are available in the real estate market. There is no international brand where you can go live anywhere in the world. There's no way of knowing how much more expensive a walk-in closet is versus not having a walk-in closet. Yeah, basically the upgrade aspect of it. Like I said, there's no international brand that you know is safe, right? There's no way of knowing how much the house behind me is in comparison to the house next to me. Those types of things are changing and as the real estate market becomes more democratized it'll just benefit consumers.

Christine: I love it. And I love industry disruption. You probably already know this number, real estate's a 200 trillion dollar industry. It's like, who can come in and exactly what you just said, create that infrastructure on a global level. Because you're right, Starbucks, anywhere you go you know what you're going to get, you know how much it is, you can pay with an App on your phone, which I do. I mean, they've made it so seamless and how do you do that with real estate and not have these crazy credit checks, and income verifications, and background checks. How do you make all that so user friendly, like push of a button. Because nowadays, especially the millennials, and we had one stay here, I'm going to interview him when he's back, he literally has a backpack and he's just randomly staying at Airbnbs, staying at people's houses, and he's jumping from different cities and different states. I actually have a couple of friends doing this right now as we speak. There's no plan, and then they do, they end up staying at some weird places.

....

Website: outpost-club.com

Head to our YouTube channel (Kindred Quarters) to watch the full interview video where Jacob also gives us a full tour of the home!

Interview with Daniel Beck | Founder of Coliving.com

Christine: Okay. Hey guys, I am here with Daniel Beck. He is the founder of coliving.com. Super excited to have him on this interview. What's fun is we actually connected back in Bali back in April, we got to meet in person. And I'm really excited, because what Daniel spent the last few years building out from scratch, which he will tell you how much work it is, is he's actually built a platform similar to Airbnb, but it's coliving.com, and it's where he's, literally, listing all the coliving homes around the world. So, you can go to that site and you can search, and you can find an amazing place to stay, to live, whether it's nightly, weekly, monthly. Our Los Angeles home, here at Kindred Quarters, is listed on the platform ourselves. So yeah, I'll go ahead and hand it over to Daniel with coliving.com. Why don't you tell us more about how long ago you started, how many years have you've been in the coliving industry?

Daniel: Thank you Christine. I started in 2014, kind of randomly. Used Airbnb to find a cheap place to stay, and I ended up being in a coliving space. It's called HackerHome Menlo Park. And I immediately loved being in this kind of like-mindedness. Other people that were in the same situation as me, and we hit it off and I started doing research what this kind of theme, or niche, was. And I found out it was called coliving. And I offered the domain owner to buy it and he wanted $10,000 and I said, "I can't give you that, but I can give you $3,000". And I bought the first domain in 2014. And, after that, I just opened up a simple email collector function and then a Wordpress version of the site came up in 2015. Didn't do very much. Didn't give an income. And then I rebuilt everything from scratch from late 2016. Used half a year by myself and then I hired my first two developers in Vietnam. They're still with me today and the website is rocking. So, we have the booking functions up and running. We're earning money. Paying bills and we trying to collect as many coliving spaces as possible. So, we have about 300 right now and there's still hundreds left to add, so we're going to be there at some point.

Christine: And do you go out and do you personally reach out to these new ones? Because there's so many new ones popping up every day now. Do you personally reach out? Do you have a system for that on how you get them on your platform?

Daniel: Yeah. All the time. We call, we email, we Facebook them, we do any communication channel you can think of and, at some point, they need to not ignore us anymore and say, "Okay, let's try this out," because it's free to add and we charge when we send bookings. So, it's a small fee, so everyone's happy. And we can still pay our bills and do marketing. So, they try out. They see that it works and they continue using us.

Christine: I love it. And is there also an actual, physical app? I always use the desktop version. Do you have the App out too?

Daniel: No App yet. It will come, at some point. It's still a lot of development on the desktop. So, I would say, maybe half a year to one year from now. No funding. It's all self-funded. I sold the previous company and using my money from that sales. And I don't want to do funding too early. Kind of gives away too much equity and control. Suddenly there's another boss. And I want to build this in my own vision and make it humane, not a big, empty, soulless company.

Christine: No, that's where me and Daniel bonded, because the same thing, which we chatted about. It was so refreshing to find somebody that's also self-funding right now when everybody's pulling, taking money. Same thing, Kindred Quarters is self-funded and it's a nice feeling to have all the control, so yeah. You're going to have different people into your home and they might not be like-minded. They might not be what you're looking for, versus an actual coliving platform and how it's a little bit different. Actually, talk about that a little bit. How is your platform different than Airbnb?

Daniel: It is different as it's more social aspect to it and we're building more and more social functions. So, you should be able to find a space based on the people living in the space. So, at some point, we want you to tell who you are and then we find that space that you should live in. On Airbnb you choose price and location and then you end up somewhere. We don't want the random part. And when people ask I say, "It's like Airbnb, just for coliving". So, it's the simplest idea. We collect money. We keep the money escrow on third party services. We don't have access to that money until it's been split between us and the host. So, people are supposed to find, book, and pay coliving spaces where we are the professional level on top of the coliving space. So different coliving spaces might have different ways of collecting payments. And we try to professionalize all that and make it easy for people. I'm not sure how much different Airbnb are or how much different we are from Airbnb, but it's easy to compare.

Christine: Awesome. And then, definitely, talk about how active you are in the business. And I know you're working crazy hours, so maybe just talk a little bit about that. It's exciting to be able to interview somebody on the development side and the software side of coliving.

Daniel: It's still early. Investors just starting to look at this. Real estate developers and big owners are asking. They send in a request and saying, "Hey, I heard of this and how can I start?" And they ask if I want to take over their property and I'm like, "I'm not doing physical spaces. You need to contact some local coliving company and ask if they can manage your space". So still, people don't know what it is. It's like, people now know what Airbnb is. You don't need to explain it to anyone. People know what home sharing is. People know what vacation rental is. At some point, there will be, "Oh, it's like coliving. So, we have one down the street," or "I lived in one and I can recommend it to everyone because you meet new people. You can talk about your passions all day instead of this random home sharing". So it's, kind of, like home sharing, but bigger and more professional. So, home sharing. Everyone's done home sharing, after school, or before school, or at school, where they share with three or four other people. But we don't have the same interests and who's doing the cleaning? This coliving is much more professional and I see the progress further as coliving for this and that. So, it'll be coliving for climbers. Coliving for divers. Coliving for surfers. Coliving for startups. Coliving for hobbies and interests. It's going to be based in different places around the world, based on what that place is meant for, like a good place for kiting, a good place for diving. So, if you have your, kind of, online business with you and you can stay for a month or longer, people would love to move into coliving space and instantly connect with the community there. And there will be so many services attached to coliving, like anything around finding a place, and also cleaning services, mainly based on coliving spaces, and yeah. So much stuff is going to come.

Christine: Yeah. What's been the most unique concept you have on your platform that you've seen so far?

Daniel: I'm not sure. I think everyone is unique in their way. A coliving different on another coliving living space is maybe the community in it. The feeling you get when you get in. Some coliving spaces does not have the community feeling to it. So, I fell in love with HackerHome Menlo Park. The original one. Yeah. It's like your first love. And I went back four times to the same place. There was different people, but they're lifelong friends. And some of them met other from that HackerHome from earlier through me. And I just love being in that area. I love the kind of people that house attracts. And I'm not sure if I ever going to have the same feeling again, because now you're used to it. So I've traveled and seen different coliving spaces, but I don't see the future of coliving as bunk beds. There might be a cheap, like one or two bedrooms in the house, maybe having bunk beds, but it's not for long-term. You can stay for a couple weeks and then you need to have your private space. So, it's a lot of coliving spaces with bunk beds and they might suffer, in a while, when more professional comes in with single and it's almost the same price and then they need to change.

Christine: No, you're right. I'm so glad you talked about it because I think that would be a different model. I think you're exactly right. And then, I stayed at the original Epic Entrepreneur House in San Diego last week. So, when I'm in San Diego, because I'm also often in L.A., I stay at that home. Again, different people, but same energy, same values. Once you create that home, it seems like that stays, even if different people move in and move out. That same energy.

Daniel: That's true. You come to a company that has a toxic culture and even though you try to change out some of the culture, once you come back again, it's like, some people are always dragging other people in. And if you have a positive start and some people are staying for long-term, they're going to transfer their positivity. So, it can change the whole amount of people there, but it's not going to change the culture in the house.

Christine: Yeah. And the energy. And I know, again, your platform is pretty new, so you probably don't have a lot of data quite yet. But, so far, what's the average stay you've noticed being booked?

Daniel: We book a lot of from one to three months. We changed our concept about two, three months ago, where we used to show nightly prices. And it's easier to see the nightly and compare it, but it's also tells people that they think they can stay for nightly. And I would never recommend anyone staying for under a week. So we changed it over to be monthly, so everything is compared on monthly now.

Christine: Good to know. So, one to three months is pretty average?

Daniel: Yeah. So, you can go in and you could stay for a week, but on top, to begin with, you will see the monthly price. And, when you choose the week, you will see the price for that week, so that everything is based on monthly. And it's because I don't think community is built on short-term. You need to come in. You need to know people. You need to know their stories. It takes maybe a couple weeks. And then, if I was staying for a couple days, I wouldn't know who you are and what you actually do, and then you leave. And also, the community in the house, when you have someone staying for short-term, you're like, "That person I don't know and that person's staying for two weeks. Should I leave my computer on?" So, if you stay for a month, it might cost more for staying there than actually stealing some computers. In an Airbnb if there's one person renting a place, it's easy to blame the person. It's like, "That happened while you were there. It must be your fault". In a coliving space, you have the whole community taking care of everyone. So everyone watches out. Everyone sees and is like, "Hey, you shouldn't leave that out". Or like, "Why do you light a fire? It can burn down the curtains". But also, if something happens in the kitchen and there's 10 people there, how can you blame one person? S, coliving spaces are professional hosts or managers and professional renters. So, I didn't see the reason to start paying someone to put in an insurance. That would also cost much more for the end-user, in a way and, yeah.

Christine: Exactly. On our first phone conversation, a while back was, technology in the homes. Talk a little bit about that. Like you said, if it's a large home and somebody's using the bathrooms, what if there's a light in each bedroom? So, if the red light says, "Oh, somebody's in the restroom, you don't need it. Somebody's using it already". What are some tech ideas you have in these smart homes?

Daniel: I think you've kind of touched my main thing there, showing in a bedroom if the shower is available before you put on your towel and start walking out. So, I made the guide of how to start a coliving business on my website and one of the things are hardware and software. And hardware is like, you cannot copy 20 keys give everyone a key and then a key is lost and then you need to find out how to copy another one. You need to make that simpler. You need to have either cards that are simple to print out or phone apps that can actually open the door. And having a heater that change based on how many people are there or that's, kind of, just setting a heater to 23 Celsius and it will always stay at 23. And there are always going to be people in the room so, it might be a couple hours in the night that it's going down. So, I'm not setting heaters and stuff like that to save energy. I think coliving is so efficient in terms of use of energy and water, if you have the right water. It's many more people using less space. And starting to do too much of trying to save a little water here and electricity there, I don't think that's where it is. It becomes more annoying, maybe, for the people living there, than what you gain from it. Software-wise is like communication in a house. It should have a Slack channel. Slack is kind of new and not everyone knows what it is. So, you might have half of the house on Slack and half not, and still you need to message the rest of them. So, Facebook groups. There's probably just going to be one or two, definitely, that is not on Facebook or hate it. And it's not easy, but you need to find the channels of software to communicate inwards. And then outwards, for the coliving space to be on as many listing sites as possible, so they can get all its leads coming in and, kind of, filter out who's good or not.

Christine: Yeah. No, I love it. Again, it gives people seeing or reading this interview ideas for their own homes, which I appreciate. And then, so my last question for you is, what's the future for coliving.com, your platform?

Daniel: I know that we're early and I was, kind of, a visionary when I discovered coliving back when no one knew what it was. I think there was one article that year about coliving and now it's thousands of articles about it and it's just four years ago, so it's a short while. But the future of coliving.com would be faster, better matching, delight to use, and to find the perfect space, of course. We're thinking about adding other functions, so you can find a job in a coliving space. If there's anyone that needs a community manager or marketer, they can post jobs there. We're thinking about allowing investors to say that they want to invest in coliving spaces, coliving companies and they can add which category they're in, how much they want to invest and stuff. So, it will be easier to say, "Hey, I'm trying to open this in a new place or a new niche. I need investors. I'm going to search for or send a request to investors and see if they want to invest in the company". Also, owners of buildings that want to do coliving and they don't know who to call, who to contact. They can add their perfect house or building. And coliving spaces that are expanding and have money for expanding can send a request saying, "We want to open up one in Chicago". They find 24 listings there from real estate owners and send a request. So I want to do more stuff around that and even more like, you can go into a coliving space and see the whole space. You're seeing like 3D model. It's just about giving more information and safety of using the website and that your money is safe, the card is safe, you know how many people, which kind of people are staying there. So, you can prepare and say, "Oh, I'm looking for cofounders and there's a couple of designers there. Perfect. Maybe after booking I can start chatting in the group and say, 'Hey, I'm coming in two weeks. Anyone up for doing this and that?'"

Christine: That's really cool. I love how innovative you are. We always say the pioneers are the ones that get the arrows in the back, right? So, you had a interesting four years leading up to now...

Daniel: It's been interesting. I had a job before that I was CTO for another company and I sold my shares in their company and then I started doing more traveling and researching. Of course, it takes a while. As you know, it's a lot before you start earning the first cents, but it's the hurdles that's come over and to keep the engine running and now it's there. It's my full-time job and I've hired four people and we're going to be more.

Christine: I love it. And why don't we end with this? Tell them where you're originally from and tell them where you're staying right now, because you are a world traveler for sure.

Daniel: It's pretty boring, because I'm from Norway and I'm in Norway right now, so I'm not traveling anywhere. I just came back seven months in Siem Reap in Cambodia, heading then to Vietnam for a couple weeks, Chiang Mai for a month, Malaysia for three weeks, back to Chiang Mai for a month, Bali for one and a half months and then stopping in Singapore on the way back to England where my girlfriend is from. And Portugal, Croatia, and now Norway, for a little bit, and then US road trip next and meeting interesting people in US.

Christine: Great, because I know you're driving from San Francisco. If we can match it up, let's see if we can give you a tour of Los Angeles.

....

Website: coliving.com

Interview with Kyron Gosse | Futurist, FreedomCo in Bali, Indonesia

Christine: Okay, super excited to talk to this person because I haven't seen him. I think it was back in April, in Bali, is when we first met. And then Myumi was sweet enough to connect us virtually and then once I went out there we sat down, and we chatted about coliving, and this guy definitely has experience in real estate, has experience in coliving and running a home. So, yeah let's just launch right into it. So, go ahead and introduce yourself and tell everybody what you're up to.

Kyron: My name is Kyron, originally from New Zealand where I'm a property investor. The goal was always to do property to be able to pay me to go traveling. So I started traveling. I lived in the Netherlands for 10 months with my Dutch girlfriend, and then we started traveling the world with a group that would take us from city to city. We didn't last too long with that. Didn't really like it, but we're like what if instead of having the entire group going from place to place each time, what if we headed to different places where the people could come to. So, that's kind of how I got involved in coliving. I didn't even know it was called coliving back then. All I wanted was to set up a place where I could have awesome people come, stay for a while and then go to the next place. And so, set up in Bali, where I did my first attempt at coliving, I guess I'd call it.

Christine: And that was how long? Was that like a year and a half ago? How long ago was that?

Kyron: I took over January 2017.

Christine: Okay, cool. And then talk a little bit, because everybody comes to us and Kindred Quarters was contemplating doing Bali, and I loved it there. It's beautiful. But tell me about the authorities, and you have to pay off people to have parties. Didn't you say it was just super corrupt?

Kyron: It's different, it's definitely different. So, I don't think Bali was the right place to get started. Obviously with coliving and with a lot of that sort of thing, people usually pay the premium, because they wanna be living with amongst other entrepreneurs, other like-minded people, and they have everything provided for them. But Bali's so cheap anyway, and the locals would be happy to make $100, $200 extra per month, which for us it wouldn't be even worth it. I was spending 100 bucks a month on coconuts alone. And so, it made it really difficult, and then it wasn't until after I'd signed up for a year-long lease where in Bali, you pay the year in advance. So, you're dropping 30 to $50,000 on a property before you've even filled it, and then having to buy all the furniture, the sheets, the knives, spoons, that sort of thing. But given it's in Southeast Asian, there is obviously corruption there, but it's just a different way of operating. So, in Bali they have little villages which are called Benjas, and the Benja is kind of like local council. In New Zealand, or America, in normal Western countries, the council have these rules that you can go on their website and you know how the rules work, right? And if you don't follow them, the council could still come and take your house. But over there, you don't know what the rules are, and it's different from Benja to Benja. So, for example, even down to how much you pay for your rubbish, I was paying $15 a month, which I thought was relatively cheap. And then another friend's like you're paying too much. I only pay $3 per month. I'm like well who really cares? But like you were saying with the parties, we'd have a party, and they'd be like oh, you didn't tell us about the party. Well, why would I? They're like well you have a party, you have to pay us. I'm like what am I paying you for? They're like for us to come and do security and for parking. I'm like well, I don't need you to park the cars, or the motorbikes. People know how to park motorbikes. I've got staff. They could help with the motorbike parking. And so, the very first party I did, that was a complete screw up. I paid two million rupiah, which is about 150 US dollars I think. And I only had seven people come, because everybody sees all the Benja there, sitting there looking all authority wise, and little red flashing lights, and they're like yeah, no. We're not gonna go. And they turn around. So, I paid $150 for seven people to come. And it was this big joke. So, we stopped telling them, and because we're where no one really noticed, but then a little restaurant opened up across the road, and that was where the Benja used to hang out. So, if we did anything, they would always know. It's a really interesting concept. Some people liken them to the mafia. But yeah, there's so many different rules. The local council could stop the police from coming in. If they don't like you, they could make your life hell. So, I made it my mission right at start when I first met them to be friendly. I said, "Hey, I wanna be part of the community, but I'm obviously not Hindu, so I'm not gonna be sitting there giving tons of money towards all the festivals and stuff. But I don't wanna be treated just like a rich Westerner whose come in and be taken advantage of." Which I'm not sure worked.

Christine: So, fast forward to now. You went back to New Zealand, right? And tell everybody what your new project is. This is super exciting.

Kyron: So, I took everything I learned from Bali. I absolutely loved it. I could never make it work. I could never make it financially viable, but I absolutely loved it. I loved that concept of just having amazing people coming, staying in the house who are always on different projects, so you can sit down over breakfast and talk about it. I was like how do we take this to the next level? One thing I realized, one of the big problems with Bali is it's so transient. People would come for one month, two months, and you'd always be trying to fill rooms. And I think I worked out I'd ideally rather be in a place where you'd have more permanent people. People who are gonna stay there a year, two years, that sort of thing. But an interesting thing that came out of Bali is I met a friend, she came and stayed at my property actually, and we became good friends. We started working together, and then she's building a tiny house in Belgium, and I was like that's really cool. I was like I've always wanted to do these little entrepreneurial villages. Imagine a tiny house village. And so that's now what we're working on in New Zealand. We've got the building for our own tiny house. We're gonna be tiny flatmates. So, that's happening right now. We managed to get funding pretty quickly. If you wanna talk about flow, it all just happened. We pitched one investor, we got the money to build it, we got the land to put property on. My parents own an amazing piece of land right on a riverfront, two minutes kayak to a waterfall, and when we went and looked at the council, we realized we could fit about 20 tiny houses on there, and it's this amazing location where there's a lot of early retirees go to. And I was like this would be a really good place for lifestyle entrepreneurs. Not digital nomads, but lifestyle entrepreneurs. People who want to escape the hustle and bustle, can work online or run their business. It's only two and a half hours to Auckland, so if you had to go to the big city every now and then it's not too much of a mission. But just to escape, to have this amazing community around them, to be able to build their business, because the last thing I want is to end up with a trailer park where everyone's sitting around not doing anything. For me, I get really inspired by people with projects, who are out there living their life. So, that's what we're working on now.

Christine: And then, so go in a little more detail about, in your opinion, digital nomad versus lifestyle entrepreneur. What's the difference, in your opinion?

Kyron: I think the big thing... I'm gonna get a lot of hate. I've always spoken out a little bit against digital nomads. If you look at most digital nomads, most of them aren't making money. A lot of them are either living off savings, or they're moving somewhere like Bali because it's cheap. But I think there's a difference between moving somewhere simply because it's cheap. You jump on the digital nomad groups and they're like where can I live for 600 bucks in a month? And it's like why limit yourself to that? Why not say, if you're a real entrepreneur, you'd say actually I love this place. So, if it's an amazing place like that, why wouldn't you say, "Okay, what do I have to do in order earn enough money to go live in Silicon Beach?" Rather than being like oh, I only know how to make 600 bucks a month. I'm gonna go live in some shitty area where I can only afford to live 600 bucks a month and make the best out of it. So, I think that's the biggest difference between digital nomads and lifestyle entrepreneurs. The other one is a lot of digital nomads I feel are just ticking countries off. They're just traveling for travel sake. I found it really difficult to build my business when I was constantly traveling, and I was so happy when I found somewhere I could just settle down and have a base, and I'd still travel, but I'd have somewhere to call home.

Christine: No, I think you're right. And I think it's almost just for the Instagram shots, right? Oh, I'm in this country, I'm in that country. And it's exhausting for them, because a lot of them behind the scenes, it gets very isolating and exhausting, they've told me. I've known people

159

that have jumped. They'll jump every two weeks for a year, but you don't make connections when people know you're only there for two weeks. It's hard to get a deep connection, so that's interesting.

Kyron: Well, we actually had that in the end in Bali, because we ended up with a group of five to ten of us who were semi-permanent. We're going to in Bali like six months, is what it takes to be semi-permanent, right? And when you go out to a networking group, you're like oh really? We gotta do all this again? Or you go out to just a social gathering, it's like oh really? How long are you here for? And if someone said I'm here for a month, you'd probably almost wouldn't bother talking to them because it wasn't going to be of any benefit to you, you know? A month later, you're gonna be talking to somebody else.

Christine: That totally makes sense. So, your title is a futurist. You think like okay, where are we heading? There's these tiny homes on a plot of land, it's still community and they still have their privacy. I think that's amazing. When are you guys gonna officially open up?

Kyron: So, the plan for this year is to get our first tiny house to test it. So, you're speaking of futurist, it's gonna be a tiny smart passive house. So, we're installing smart systems. So, if it gets too hot, it will open the window automatically, as it starts getting later at night it'll start dimming down the lights. It'll be keyless entry, all these sorts of things. I wrote the book Future of Property, which was talking about all the different trends and technologies which were coming into place, and now this is a chance for me to actually show people what that looks like. And I talk a little bit about the convergence, which is when you have tiny houses, you have smart homes, and you have coliving, but what happens when you combine them together and you have something that's never been there before. And for me, that's what's most exciting about everything we're doing now.

Christine: That's why I'm so excited! I told him before we started, I'm like I'm so excited to talk to you again, just because it's like there's a saying that the pioneers get all the arrows in the back. You know what I mean? So, being a futurist and trying to jumpstart a trend, or just you see it, and I believe that. It's for sure going that direction. But it's like okay, we're just gonna go and figure it out. We're definitely gonna get some arrows in the back on the way, but I love that. I believe wholeheartedly in that. Especially the smart home stuff too. Our last home had some amazing technology tied into it, and it was really beneficial for everybody living there, you know? Everything was on app. It was crazy. We could heat the jacuzzi up, the pool, we could turn lights on or off, the air, everything was on app, and it was like how cool would this be if we had this at every house? Keyless entry, same thing. So, that's really cool. So, let me see. So, some of my questions, because mine are more tailored because I know what you're doing is so unique. Let's see here. What average age do you think are gonna be in those homes?

Kyron: That's a really interesting question. In Bali, I would've said between 25 and 35. My target market is still that sort of thing. It's essentially people who they get a massive student loan, go to university, come out of it, go get the job, they get the job to pay off their student loan, but they've got to live close to their job so they gotta pay really high rent in order to just go from job, and it's this vicious cycle, right? And it's like, what if you could break away from all that? The tiny house mortgage is going to be less than $100,000, to have this sweet pad that's an actual asset. Then if you wanted, you could just tow, travel the country, come back. The goal is to eventually have different villages, 10 villages around New Zealand. So, you could go from our one in Auckland down to our one in Wellington and live there for six months. That's what the eventual goal is. But that's really who it is. It's about getting people away from getting a massive student loan, going into a job that they hate, and becoming what I call a corporate zombie. It's about how do you actually find your passion, follow your passion, how do you find your purpose, and how do you tie it all in together so that you're not doing the Monday to Friday, go to your work, come home, sit in traffic, watch TV, veg out, until you have to get up in the next morning and sit in traffic to go to your job. Because when people come alive, and they find something that they love, it's like a crusade right? When they find a crusade that they're willing to stand up for, fight for and drive, it doesn't matter what it is, you can see the passion in someone's eyes and it inspires everyone.

Christine: Oh my gosh, I love that. And then where are you staying at? So, you're back in New Zealand now, and where do you live? Who do you live with now? Do you have any coliving situation you're doing right now?

Kyron: Well, this is funny, because I was only supposed to be coming back for two months. I came back just to see what was happening in the property market. I make most of my money through property investing still, so I came back to see what was happening, and then like I said, just everything fell into place. The tiny house stuff fell into place, the investing has all fallen into place, and I was like oh, I gotta figure everything out. We were booking flights back to Bali, and I was like what am I even going back to Bali for? My lease is up, I'd literally be flying there to pick up some clothes I left there, which are worth less than 300 bucks, and the flight would be 1000. And so, right now I'm just staying in a friends' place. I'm house sitting. She went to America for a month. I was like that's perfect. I'll stay, look after your place. So, there's gonna be about a month in between when she comes back, and the tiny house is finished. So, I'll be doing a bit of couch surfing, or I do have a friend, he doesn't quite run coliving spaces as we would know them, but he does have a couple of investment properties that he rents out to a private room. So, I could potentially go into that sorta situation.

Christine: I love that. And then so that's kinda your future, that's what's going on with what you're doing, which is super exciting. My last question with every interview is where do you see the industry of coliving in general? Where do you see that going?

Kyron: I think we're right at the start of it. So, coliving fits into what I would call housing as a service. So, obviously we started out when things like Uber came along. We've got transport as a service. We're definitely moving into a space where it's housing as a service, because there are a lot of people out there, and it's right at the start, right? Where people are like you know what? I don't need to buy a house. Personally, I've never wanted to own my own home. I've bought hundreds of properties, but I've never, ever bought my own home. So, this tiny house will be my first ever home. And the problem is, if you buy a home you're stuck with it. So, I think we're right at the cusp of housing as a service. Airbnb started a lot of that, coliving has taken it to the next level, and we're going to start to see a few different things. Coliving can be broken down into a domestic market where it's mainly people from that country. Like in America, right? The coliving industry in America is predominantly Americans living in a property with other Americans. Whereas when you look at the more traditional nomad hot spots, they're travelers. So, you've got the domestic market, and you've got the foreign market. So, we're gonna see different things happening within both sides of it, but I think we're gonna start to see alliances forming, and you've obviously talked to the coliving hub, the guys from there? Or you will be?

Christine: Yeah, I will be. Yeah.

Kyron: Yeah. So, I helped start that conversation, but where suddenly rules are forming, what does coliving even entail, what are the basic standards that other people are gonna have to meet if you come up to it, and much like we had in the backpacker, or hostel industry where you have all the little independents, which would've been formed under one sort of alliance so that they could get more business, they could set the standards and people would know what they'd be coming into. I think we'll start to see a lot of that happening. The big thing about coliving is there's no real barrier to entry. So, I think we'll see a lot of coliving spaces pop up fast once someone gets that particular model right.

Christine: I haven't checked in the last month, is there an association yet for coliving, or no? I know there's a few for coworking.

Kyron: Not that I know of. I'd say Coliving Hubs are the closest to an association.

....

Website: facebook.com/freedomcoglobal

163

Interview with Avi Mermelstein | Cofounder & CEO of here&now in New York

Christine: Perfect, I have Avi here. And I'm so excited. I love his website, I love the verbiage, I wrote down one of the quotes on the website. It was cracking me up. It's like crushing the rules of an archaic rental system, which is so true with property management, it is archaic. And also on your LinkedIn it's like, "Have fun, get shit done, make a difference." I love it. So touch on that, touch on the brand first off and tell me how you guys got started.

Avi: So my experience is in real estate development. We've been developing multifamily for about four years now. Loved what I was doing, but got to a point where I said, "Hey what am I really doing to better people's lives?" We're just building straight multifamily products, which is super nice, but how can we have an impact? I kind of did a lot of soul searching and researching, and I found the coliving concept, the whole world then. I fell in love with it, it gets to combine real estate and building communities. And I think building communities really has such an impact on people's lives. And that's how I got into it originally. And the more I get into it, the more doors open, and I'm seeing how it's amazing how much of an impact we could have as a space.

Christine: That's awesome. Do you guys have a cofounder?

Avi: I do have a cofounder, he's actually my business partner. We have two founders, Jack and Kailey. Jack also has real estate experience, and Kailey comes from the art scene. So it's super collaborative, and it's great.

Christine: Love it. And then you said you started the concept in September, but then just opened your first location?

Avi: Correct. We just opened our first location in Birchwood, Brooklyn. Super exciting. We've been working on the brand for about a year, and just trying to figure out, again people throw around the world coliving so much now. But we really wanted to figure what about coliving we wanted to do. How do we want to bring people together? I think when we talk about creating communities, there has to be that common thread that weaves through everyone that really brings people together. And we kind of landed on social impact, on having fun, getting shit done, and making a difference. And that's where we ended up.

Christine: I love it. And then how many people can stay at your first location at a time?

Avi: 18 people.

Christine: Oh, 18. Nice that's a good amount of people. And do you personally live in the concept?

Avi: I do. It's amazing, it's so much fun. And I get to meet amazing people. And yeah, I hope to always live there.

Christine: I know right? I live in mine too, so it's fun. And then how active are you, like what's your day to day role in the business?

Avi: I want to be very active. I think it's extremely important. Everyday I'm speaking to people, I'm always trying to get feedback. The most important times I believe are during dinners when everyone is hanging around, and at night when everyone's getting back from work, getting back from their busy day and just want to talk, want to get to know the new people. And I think that's the most important. But every day I'm speaking to people, we're looking at new locations. We're speaking to local businesses to see how we can create more of a presence in the community. And, yeah.

Christine: That's awesome. So do you guys just do month to month, what's the bare minimum stay?

Avi: We wanted to make it more convenient for everyone, so we didn't require such a long lease. We did want to create that sense of community, so we wanted to do a little longer. We didn't want to do nightly, we think to really create community takes time. To really build relationships, you have to have conversation after conversation.

And that's the beauty of it. So we're doing a minimum of four months, but we have people staying up to a year.

Christine: And then do you have separate a coworking space designated in the house?

Avi: Correct. So the top three levels are all residential, the apartments where everyone lives. And then the downstairs we converted into a coworking space/common lounge with little nooks for everyone to do their work.

Christine: I love that, that's awesome. And then what is your favorite part about running the coliving home?

Avi: It's about opening your eyes to so many different experiences, meeting so many different people. We all think we have all the answers, then you go speak to someone who comes from, who has a software development background. And they give you this completely new insight on the real estate sector. And you're like I never knew you could bring that much technology into an industry that's been doing the same thing for 50, 60 years. And that's the most beautiful thing, you have so many different people with so many different backgrounds just collaborating, that's my favorite part.

Christine: I saw that you guys partnered with Casper. That company is blowing up in the mattress space, I can't believe it. How did that partnership start?

Avi: So again, got on the phone with them, told them about what we were doing, and they loved it. And they were super open to it, and it's been a great partnership. We've also partnered with Brooklyn Bicycles, which is a local biking company here out in Brooklyn. So it's a way for everyone to get around Birchwood. We actually have bikes in the spaces for everyone to get around, which has been amazing. And yeah, we're also partnered with Rhino, an insurance startup. People who can put down deposits, or people who want to, so it's like a kind of an insurance company for deposits.

Christine: Okay. And then the gym, don't you guys have gym membership too?

Avi: Yeah, so we're working on that right now. It's a little tricky legality, but we're working on it.

Christine: Nice. Making everybody in shape together. So it's motivating, for sure. And then what kind of events do you guys do?

Avi: So every Sunday night we have a dinner. Kailey, which is one of the cofounders, when she came to New York she didn't know so many people. So she started this thing where kind of a dinner every Monday night where she would invite random people off the street and Ubers to come to their dinner in groups of 30 people. We loved it, and we started doing this here now. And we have tons of different people coming in, it's so exciting. And so that's one of the staples, every Sunday night there's always dinner. We always invite people to come by and just have dinner. It's a lot of fun. And then we have usually one monthly event. Something more of like an excursion, something for everyone to kind of get out.

Christine: Cool. And you guys have a good turnout from the residents?

Avi: Yeah. Everyone loved the dinners, again everyone loves food. We all love food, you can't go wrong. We provide the food. For guests who come, we always ask for a contribution, because sometimes if there's a lot of people it can get a little expensive. So whatever you can give to the table would be much appreciated. But we do provide them food.

Christine: Cool. And then what is your guys' resident demographic? Like the age, is it mostly guys, is it girls?

Avi: Right now it's fairly even split. I would say 60% guys, 40% girls, anywhere the ages of 20 to early 40's. Yeah, lots of different backgrounds. It's been amazing.

Christine: And then do most of them work there in New York? Or are they digital nomads, are they business owners?

Avi: Yeah, so we are completely all over the spectrum. We have an actor, who is actually right now on a cruise acting. He is going to come back hopefully in two weeks. We have someone in educational technology, real estate developer. We have a DJ, we have a vegan chef, and that's the coolest part. Again, it's whatever you can think of.

Christine: Okay, cool. That's super cool. And then what's the future you guys have? What's your growth plan? Have you guys taken any seed money, any financing to start? Do you guys have locations scouted already for the future?

Avi: Yes, so we're self-funded for right now. We're kind of piggy backing off the multifamily business, which was we raised from family and friends and we said, "Hey we really love this coliving concept. We'd love to give it a try. Let us try it, worst case scenario, you can go back to multifamily traditionally." But we love this concept, and we're already looking at other locations in Brooklyn. And hopefully down the road we want to keep it very lean as possible. We really want to focus on building a great community. And I think to do that, we have to be really hands on in management, and management intensive. And really get to know the people, we can't just throw money at that, right? That's speaking to the people, it's all about building relationships, and we're going to take our time.

Christine: Cool, I love hearing that. Yeah, I'm in a similar boat right now. Just starting it slow, and then we can inject capital in once we've kind of got our footing. So my last question, the most important, is what do you feel like is the future for coliving as an industry?

Avi: I think many people thing coliving is just about creating community, and that's I think one of the best aspects. But I think for me it's also about streamlining and making the rental process seamless. So instead of meeting a broker on a random corner and you have to put down a deposit in the next five minutes, or someone else is going to grab it and making it such a stressful and hectic process. I really think coliving is also about bringing that Zappos, bringing that Amazon experience to real estate. Really focusing on the customer and not focusing on the landlord's pocket. It's not about how much financing they could pull out, but more what experience we're giving to the people who are living in these communities. And how do we enrich their lives? How do we help them spend their money in a more efficient way? Are they going to spend $2,000 on a couch, or are they going to use that money to go travel to South America for a few weeks? So it's about really empowering people, and helping them to use their money to enrich their lives.

Christine: Do you have a heavy property management or real estate background?

Avi: We do. So yeah, I've been in development for a few years. My business partner is in development as well, but he has a property management background. But we've been learning a lot as we go along. It's been an amazing process, and we're learning every day.

Christine: You talk like you're a veteran, that's why I asked. Because you're right, it's such an old industry that needs disruption. That's why I'm so excited. It's like Uber did it with the taxis, and Airbnb is doing it with hotels.

Avi: And it should be about the tenants right, it should be about the people living there right?

Christine: Yeah. Awesome Avi, thank you so much for doing this interview with us. We're super excited to get this movement going for coliving, get that word out there.

....

Website: herenowliving.com

Interview with Elaine Wong | Cofounder of The Hatchery Place in Malaysia

Christine: Okay, I am here with Elaine. She's out in Malaysia which is really cool and she has The Hatchery Place that she's gonna tell us all about. I was already spying on them on their Instagram page. I know I'm gonna go into depth and ask her about some of their cool events that they've hosted lately, so Elaine, go ahead and let us know about your coliving home out there like how long you've had it and how many people live there, all that fun stuff.

Elaine: I'm Elaine and I started this place, The Hatchery Place, together with my partner Kevin who is not here today because he's pretty busy. We started here since 2016 in February and we have ran this place since then and we have never stopped ever since. We started it with the intention to have a creative and conscious coliving plus coworking space for the local people here and also for the travelers. We have always dreamed to have this space for ourselves and also to share with other people and so our dream came through in 2016. We dared to quit our corporate together at the same time in order to do this, but it's also for the rest of the people who are inclined to join us, too.

Christine: I love that, and then were you guys already in Malaysia or did you live somewhere else?

Elaine: I lived in Germany for four years during my corporate years and then because of the money that I had saved when I was overseas, I decided to come back here with my little savings to start this place together because we do need a little bit of capital before we can venture into this risk. I would call this a risk.

Christine: Did you have to a long-term lease? Did you have to furnish it? What kind of things did you guys have to do?

Elaine: We do sign a lease. Our landlord already knows what we are doing because we had a tough time explaining to him what we were gonna do with his house, but he's very open to this concept, so thank you landlord. And we had to buy some second-hand furniture in order to start it off and at the same time, we build our furniture using the recycled pallet wood from places we can get and other people who donate to us and so we had some volunteers coming in exchange for accommodation. They help us to build the furniture here, so it's pretty awesome then we started.

Christine: Oh, I love that. That's really cool. It's almost like trade to stay type of thing. You and Kevin personally live in the home, too, right, obviously?

Elaine: We do have a room to ourselves where I paint because I converted one to be my painting studio, so sometimes we do stay here together with our coliving folks. Otherwise, we are only staying across the road. That's where our own house is, so it's very easy for us to come over. We pop by every day to manage the place.

Christine: Then, how many people can stay in your coliving home at a time?

Elaine: As much as five at a time because we only have two little rooms for people to stay in upstairs and downstairs is where the coworking space and all the creative activities are held. We have three rooms upstairs. One I use for my other studio and so there's two more rooms there, so at one time we can house as much as five persons.

Christine: Do people share rooms? Is there bunk beds? Is there two beds?

Elaine: You can share them room if you want to. Otherwise, we will have to take one person in one room. We have a single bed in one of the rooms and another one is a double bed and then we have extra mattresses in our store room for anyone who wants to have a tighter living situation, so we can cater to that, and in our own house which is just opposite the road, we also have a spare room, so it become a very big plush family staying together when we have a lot of bookings.

Christine: Nice. Okay, I love that. Then, how much time do you think spend working on the coliving home? Is it like a full-time job?

171

Elaine: It has become my full-time job because I do pop over here every single day including Saturday and Sundays because it has been a part of my life. It's my life's goal that we have created here as much as Kevin's, so both of us would come here daily and we work on our stuff together with the coliving folks here, so we will be working and then when it's time for a meal, we'll go out together and when it's time for a break, we will have fun and have some drinks together and have a movie night together. Then in the weekends, we run workshops, creative workshops. We have drum circles every month, little mini drum circles. It's really fun. I love them. I always look forward to it and then I teach painting workshop in the weekend and then we have other facilitators which is the local people that we invite them to come here to hold workshops so everyone can benefit from it, the people who coworkers here and also the people who colive here.

Christine: That is so cool. I love that you guys did a Kombucha workshop, it looks like, and garden...

Elaine: Yes, we have it monthly, too.

Christine: Where do your guests travel from? Where are most of them from?

Elaine: All over the world. We have been having some Australians lately, but we do have other European people like from France, from Germany, even had one from Estonia, from UK, as far as Brazil. I can't remember. Oh, we had one checked out from Japan, so it was so cool. We also have local people. You will be surprised. They want to try coliving concept and because I think we are the first one here in Malaysia and there are two more popping up, so I guess we are still a new concept in Malaysia so the locals do come over and try to stay with us for a week to experience everything.

Christine: What's your minimum stay? Can people stay per night, per week, per month, anything?

Elaine: Minimum just a week, so people can actually try to invest in a week's experience and if they like it, they can always lengthen your stay provided we have availability. On average, it's like two to three weeks.

Christine: Okay, that's good. What are the average ages of the people?

Elaine: I think it's mostly like early 30s or late 20s, but I do have people like my age. We're in our early 40s.

Christine: And that's about the range that everybody's pretty much at is what we're hearing. Then, what's the future for your home? What do you guys see? What's your plan? Do you plan on expanding to more locations?

Elaine: Yes. We're still pretty happy doing our things here because we like our own art and crafts. Kevin has been doing woodworking since he quit his corporate job with the central bank, so from a banker and a web designer, he has become a woodworker because of our place here and for me myself, I'm still gonna pursue my lifelong dream to be a full-time artist which I've already done it for the past three years and I'm still going forward to that, so our dream for The Hatchery Place. We call it The Hatchery Place 2.0 which is actually in our dream list. We want it to have a bigger space, but still based in Malaysia where we can accommodate all that we want. For example, we need space for our yoga. Right now, we can only do meditation here on a small scale, but we can't do too much here.

Christine: Yeah. Oh, nice. Then my last question is what do you see the future of coliving as an industry worldwide? What do you see the future?

Elaine: I think this is coming up more and more and people, not only young people. Of course, the young people do catch up with trends first, but I believe people like me, we're growing old. We're going to our 50s in less than decade's time and we need to have this kind of coliving concept to grow old happily for me. That's what I think because looking at the old folks here now, they tend to grow old alone which is, yeah, kind of sad because they don't know how to find their own community as they age and friends do pass away, so I think coliving concept, we have to embrace it at this time at this current trend and continue to embrace it and not only things that this concept is only for the millennials or for the young people. It's for everyone. Yeah, I think we have been doing this since ages ago. It's just people as time pass, they just live in isolation and now we're back to living in a community.

Christine: You're right Elaine, that's such a great point to end on. I appreciate that, because I've been saying that, too. We started as tribes and then you're right. I don't know what happened where everybody kind of became more isolated, but then now I think people got too isolated so now they're seeking community again.

Elaine: Yes. Exactly. Exactly that.

Christine: Oh, that's awesome. Well, thank you so much for taking the time today on this interview. I really appreciate it. You did great and I'm so excited to get coliving out there more to the public and if I'm ever out in Malaysia I will definitely come by.

....

Website: thehatcheryplace.com

Interview with Rolf Oftedal & Stian Morel | Cofounders of Arctic Coworking Lodge in Lofoten, Norway

Christine: Okay you guys, we're going to go ahead and get started. Really exciting, because both of the founders are on. And they own Arctic Coworking Lodge over in Norway. And so we haven't had anybody from Norway yet either, so I'll go ahead and let each of them introduce themselves and tell you guys about their concept.

Stian: I'm Stian. I'm 25 years old. I love to surf and be in the mountains.

Rolf: And I'm Rolf. I'm 24 years old and me and Sean moved up here to Lofoten to start this coliving space. Because we thought it was a really good idea and something that we will see a lot more of in the future.

Christine: And how long ago did you guys start?

Rolf: September was when we started. Last year was when we started to map out the project. We found this house in the middle of January and we opened the first of June.

Christine: June of this year? Oh, you guys are brand new! That's awesome. How many people can stay at a time?

Rolf: Twelve people. Yes, so we have eight dorm beds and two private rooms.

Stian: Our dorm beds are kind of like capsules, so we kind of designed them so you have more room in the capsule. Even though it's a dorm.

Christine: Perfect. And I've got to tell everybody seeing this, you guys have an amazing video on your home page, if they go to your website. So beautiful there. So you guys can literally surf and snow ski at the same. Is that what I'm seeing?

Stian: Yes, we can surf in the Mountains and then ski down the same day kind of thing.

Christine: What part of the year can you do that, typically? How many months out of the year?

Rolf: The thing in summer is that you have endless daylight. But the thing you have in winter is that there's almost no daylight. So in January, you probably can't ski and snowboard in the same day. You probably have to choose because there's not enough daylight to do it. But when you hit April and May, then you suddenly have the best of both worlds. Where you have almost endless daylight and you have snow and you have surf and whatever you want to do. You can climb, you can hike, you can pretty much everything.

Christine: So it looks like perfect destination for people who are into adventure sports and into surfing. Is it mostly play or is there still a lot of work going on in your space?

Rolf: There's still a lot of work. People come here because of necessity. They need a place to work.

Stian: I think we see every day, because they have been working every day like a normal job. They do their hours when it suits them and then they play. But it's definitely a lot of work.

Rolf: The most important thing is to find the right balance. To be able to work as much as be as productive as you can. And still be able to go play.

Christine: So do you see them breaking their day up? Or do they typically work like a Monday-Friday, 8-5? Do they still work 40 hours a week, I guess?

Stian: It depends on the money. There's always a lot of different people. We had a ghost writer here the last month. And the only thing he was tied up to was client phones or phone calls with new clients. So that guy, the only thing he was tied up to was phone calls with his clients. And then he kind of broke up his writing whenever he wanted to. Then we have one that was more like of working 8-2 or 8-3 every day. So it's different personalities. But we see they talk a lot together. One was reading. The other stops to proof. And they're working altogether.

Christine: Oh, that's cool. And you guys have different cultures there, right? So what's your demographic? You have people from around the world, but what's the demographic of the people who stay there?

Rolf: I think they are half Norwegians and a couple from the UK and one American.

Stian: There's one American coming in a few days. We've heard that it's really developed in America.

Christine: And then, how do people find you? Again, you guys just opened, so is it just word of mouth right now?

Rolf: Pretty much word of mouth, I guess. Instagram, Facebook. Pretty much there. We try to post a lot of content there.

Stian: We've done a few stunts with marketing. Which gave us a few bookings. Like the opening stunt. We had an opening that was pretty cheap, to get people here. And then the kind of word of mount has started a little bit.

Rolf: But that is the challenge for coliving spaces is, how do you market yourself? If you're a regular hostel, then you can just put yourself on Booking.com and get free bookings for 50% of the sum. But that's hard when you don't have those established players in coliving guests.

Christine: We had him on already for an interview! Daniel Beck of Coliving.com. Have you seen his software? Are you guys listed on there?

Rolf: Yes, we are listed on there. He is Norwegian as well.

Christine: So I know he's just now getting bookings. Which is exciting. So I think you're right. That will change it and make it a lot easier for people to book.

Stian: It just needs a little bit of punch, because it's still a pretty fresh thing to do, coliving. Next to staying at a hostel.

Christine: And that's one of my questions for you guys later on. Let's see, you guys both live in the concept also, right? You live there?

Rolf: No, Stian actually lives in a caravan outside.

Stian: Because houses are really hard to find during the summer. Because everybody wants to rent them out for Airbnb. I have a caravan outside of the space, but I try not to be... I don't want to live in the concept.

Christine: Oh, why is that, out of curiosity?

Rolf: I think it's because we want it to be a place of business for us as well. Not more like a home. Because in the past we have tried the Airbnb thing. And had people come live in the home where you also are living. And it's kind of a little bit of conflict of interest, I think. You don't have that same work mentality when you go in there. So when I go in there, it's like we need to clean this, we need to clean this, and look at this. And go in there with work, that you're taking care of the space and not necessarily living there yourself and using it and consuming it, I guess.

Christine: Great point. And it's kind of like a 50/50 split right now. But if you had asked me a month ago, everybody that I talked to, nobody lived in their concept. But then on these interviews, it's like a 50/50 split. I currently live in the concept and I have the whole time. But I can see, it's definitely different, just like you said.

Stian: I think it changes a lot about where you are and how you define your concept. Especially here, it's pretty far away from a lot of things. So it needs to be a bit different. There's a lot of things to be done and if you are always there, you can't be off. But I think it's good to be there and do the marketing work and all those things. Hang out there. Make food and hang out, but having your own private space is nice.

Christine: That makes sense. So do you guys host events there yet?

Rolf: We are thinking about having a photo course in September.

Stian: There's also an art festival that we're booking for next summer. So I think we are going to start developing a lot of different events as long as we go. We haven't had any. We have had a few parties. We had an opening party and people coming here to hang out. But we are probably going to do something a little bit more legitimate, like events, and try to market them a bit in the future.

Christine: I know you just opened so it's probably hard to think. But what's the future? What do you guys see? Multiple locations, do you see expanding the current location or keeping it as is?

Rolf: We have the possibility because this property consists of three houses. And we use half of one house right now. So we have the possibility to expand in the future. But first, we need to fill up the twelve spaces we have and then we can see the possibility to expand. I think it would be cool to try to open more locations as well. But it's kind of hard to think forward right now.

Stian: I think it's really important to have the quality in mind. And try to learn as much as possible in this kind of period. Know what needs to be done and not need to be done. And not think too much about expanding now. But try to learn and make something really good and sustainable.

Rolf: Because that's the hard part for us. Me and Stian, we love evolving projects. We love taking it from nothing and expanding it into something else. But it's kind of harder for us. Especially now at the beginning to kind of take care of the space and do all the routine work when we're not really settled into that mentality yet. So I think that's the hard part for us right now.

Christine: My last question, and the most important, is where do you see the future of coliving as an industry? Where do you see it going?

Rolf: I think we're going to see a lot more of it. And I think we're just in the beginning phase of the coliving. We have the early adopters. We don't have mass market going into coliving spaces yet. Most people don't really know what it is. Especially here in Norway. So we get a few weird looks when we say we have a coliving space. They're like, "Coliving? What's that?" That's what's happening here. But I'm guessing in the US, it's different. And we can kind of see what happens in the US. Give it a few years and it will start to happen the same in Europe as well, I think.

Stian: And there's a really big thing going on with Facebook. How it's kind of taken over the whole marketing scene, almost. It's taken a big part and there's a lot of stuff happening with internet and being remote. In my eyes, a huge thing going on. Which all kind of points into this. And how, bus tourism, you don't see that too much here in Norway. There's more of a reason to go.

Rolf: For us, we're seeing that there is a new tourism market there. Okay, I can use coliving to have people in big cities live more cost efficient. That's a good way to see coliving. For us, in our perspective, it's a little different. Because we're a tourist destination. Lofoten is not a hard place to find a place to live. Or it's expensive. We don't solve those problems, but what we're doing is giving remote workers a community to stay at if they want to come. And I think that's what's going to drive the coliving. Our little segment or branch of coliving, that's the people are going to start working more remotely and that's what we think.

Christine: Millennials... Is that like a term you guys use a lot too over there? Millennials? Like that age bracket?

Rolf: It's a term, but not like we use it on a daily basis. But I guess we are millennials ourselves.

Christine: And is that the age? What is the age demographic of the people that stay with you?

Rolf: Twenty to early thirties.

Christine: Okay, perfect. Awesome. Any final thoughts or anything you guys wanted to talk about?

Rolf: Come to Lofoten!

Stian: I think because we've lived here since September. And I remember when I came here, I was like, "What the actual fuck?" And now I see all of this stuff every day. There are so many changes all the time in so many magnificent ways. It's hard to say. It's local.

Rolf: It's hard to explain how beautiful it is. If you want to get inspired in a way, if you have a project that you're working on and you feel kind of stuck. And you want to have a change of scenery, this is where you should come. Because there are changes every day. And it's different from what people have experienced before.

Christine: No, I love it. And I'm so glad you guys did this interview outside. Because it's just so pretty. And like I said, your video on your website, it's gorgeous there. It's like another world. So thank you so much for taking the time to do this interview, both of you. I appreciate it. And yeah, we'll have to make it out there soon. Bye, you guys! Thank you so much.

....

Website: arcticcoworking.com

Interview with Peter Thompson | Pioneer at Haas in San Francisco

Christine: Okay, Christine here with the Coliving Code really excited to have Peter here. He is the pioneer at house in San Francisco. This is our first interview with somebody that is running this concept up in San Francisco. We know how crowded it is there. We know how housing is almost impossible to find. We've had friends that have moved up there and told us how hard it is. So Peter will definitely go into detail about his amazing project he has up there. I haven't seen it yet, but I'm excited next time I'm up there to take a look. It's home as a service, which we'll definitely dive into that topic. You guys have probably heard the acronym too, like housing as a service and just kinda similar to software as a service. Right? I think that housing and home is gonna easily be a service, not just a piece of property you buy and have a 30 year mortgage on. I don't think any of us want that really anymore. Especially this generation. So okay Peter, why don't you go ahead and tell us how you got started. Tell us more about your concept, how many locations.

Peter: For sure. So I guess the first thing is to mention like a lot of people in San Francisco I'm out of the tech sector so I'm one of, I would say my start in San Francisco came living in a hacker home. I think there's still quite a few here or startup homes, but yeah, playing off the tech plot firm idea as software as a service. You've got a lot of companies now which are based on digital platforms like Airbnb, et cetera, and so playing from that yeah, home as a service became a thing and I agree, it's really at the core of it, this is about access to home. Like we all need a safe place to come home to, to connect, to grow and it's about the people, not just the physical space, so that's kind of at the core of what we've created. I would say for me starting this. It's been a journey, for sure. Many different intersections of things I'm passionate about. But five years ago I came to San Francisco. I lived in a hacker home and I just realized how amazing it was, the kinds of minds of people you could plug into and that was really at the core of all of this, I think that's the amazing piece. Like the way we're raised and we're supposed to live and we all got our own space and we're separated. I think you miss a lot and I'm from a rural

182

farming community in a very rural part of Canada and I didn't have access to any of these things naturally, like everybody I grew up with, I'm supposed to be a farmer somewhere. So meeting these kinds of people that I was able to get, just by getting roommates, that, it's life-changing, and I think a lot of people that I've met, especially here, that's what this is. It's giving access to a life that you dream of having, but all you need to do is just change your rent into say a membership in a home. I think seeing that is where that came from. And then I'm really into sustainability, a lot of social impact issues. I also grew up in construction which comes in handy when you're building physical spaces. So for me this is an intersection in creating Haas. It's a vehicle to do a lot of good things, but really enjoy living my life while I'm doing it.

<u>Christine</u>: And then how many locations total do you guys have?

Peter: We have now three. We had been up to five sort of startup typical challenges. For about a year we were about five and 50 members. We're now scaled back to three homes, about 22-23 members on average. It's a team that lives in the home and also just regular members that have all sorts of walks of life. But yeah, three homes in the SoMa, latest home being in the Dogpatch of San Francisco.

<u>Christine</u>: Nice, and then do you live in one of the concepts also?

Peter: I do. I actually kind of float around all of the homes. Part of this, as well, is not being tethered down. This also comes from the digital nomad kind of thing, which I lived in and that's also, I guess, a big piece of this and I don't want to be locked down by a home. If I have an opportunity or experience to have I wanna have a home wherever I am, so in San Francisco we're kind of doing a beta play on that, where I've probably lived in each of the homes, and hopefully in the near future we'll have homes in a few other cities as. You get a membership, but you can go wherever you wanna be.

<u>Christine</u>: And then do you guys have a minimum, do people have to stay at least a month or is pretty flexible?

Peter: Right now we're still being pretty flexible. It's a month, but we've gone from the early days just to get things going being very Airbnb, which is nightly at times, weekly, but that's also fraught with a lot of issues. Definitely can't do it in most cities now and definitely not San Francisco, but that also doesn't lend itself to creating a real home when people are so transitional. So we do allow people to move in for a month minimum, but we hope and often we see people stay much longer and that's kind of our aim. And as we get more stable with that, we'll probably start making it harder to do the one month, under maybe more special circumstances, like for example right now, we're trying to help artists stay in San Francisco, so right now I'm actually in a collaboration house that's sort of a tech-artist collaborative where we're subsidizing artists that wanna stay. You can't be a techy making really good money and stay for a month maybe.

Christine: I think there's some mention to that somewhere on your website, right? That you guys are trying to go more toward more like anti-tech, even though your background is tech.

Peter: Yeah, yeah, I am a tech and I often joke that I'm one of the evil tech that is in San Francisco, it's almost a bad word to a lot of people outside of tech, because there's a lot of social pressures here, but it's more so that I wanna give access, like a lot of us in tech, you know, and and many people, we're from more privileged backgrounds that we were able to pursue this path and we are creating the future and we have access to the capital and the opportunities that a lot of other people are more than capable to be a part of and the truth is, we need them. Like a lot of techies forget that without human needs somewhere being addressed, what we're creating isn't orally valuable so techies benefit by meeting real people that actually live in the world and do day-to-day things like the artists, like the people at the grocery store, so I'm trying to extend what I experienced in these hacker homes and give access to people from all walks of life, so on that part of it, I think it's a way of really gluing together, helping sort of fix some of these divides we have in society. Like the artists often would be against techies and the techies against the artists. And I guess this home as an example of that. By bringing those people together we can create a future that's good for all of us, so that's kind of at the core of my mission with what I'm trying to do with this.

Christine: That's awesome. And then what's your evolution been since you started a year and a half ago? Did you have to pivot your model a few times as you went?

Peter: I don't know if the models had to pivot too much. It's been more of an experimentation of the different types of people that we've got in because I've tried to do a lot of things. I think I went a little bit too far in trying to help some people bring them into the home. Probably wasn't ready to handle some of the challenges some people have in life. So I think it's been more about learning what boundaries I have to put into place right now, in what areas. It's about focus, really, so what kind of demographics can we focus on? What kind of service can we offer right now versus what do we have to put off for the future, so the model stayed relatively the same. We probably evolved our membership guidelines and policies and experimented with different lengths. It's really building up how do we do the sales process. A lot of our homes are shared space, so it's not just living with a bunch of people and have a private room. It's like we're sharing rooms often and we're creating different types. Like, maybe they're common in Japan and maybe in hostels in Asia, but we're trying to bring some of that here because again. From the environmental perspective, we waste way too much space and most of us, we don't live in a city like San Francisco to sit in a private living room by ourselves all day or a private room, we need to sleep, so we provide private space that you can escape to. We call them sleep pods right now, but other than that, we're here to kind of meet and hang out and go explore the city and build ideas, so that is a change. We're slowly finding out who's gonna help us drive that change, get them in here first.

Christine: That's awesome. And then let's here, do you guys host events and if you do, do you let outside people come to those events?

Peter: Yes, so we do host events. It's pretty important to us to try to make sure there's collaboration across the homes. Each home has a little bit of a different vibe and type of people we try to bring in. We want these homes to be the members help create them, versus us being the top down, here's what you're gonna get. Here's your rules and what not. So we have events that are just home-specific, like home dinners and stuff like that. Really try to encourage that stuff. But then we have various activities, either out in the city or in our homes that we invite everybody from the homes, of course, but very open to anybody. They're open to anybody that wants to come. Often what we do is try to post invites to events that we're going to go as a group, or at our homes in the housing Facebook groups here in San Francisco, just to wanna get people then organically as much as possible and it's the best way to find out if you wanna live in a home or if you know, we're the right kind of people for you, is just to come hang out with us. Versus it being much more transactional, traditional business kind of process.

Christine: And then is your coworking space, is it integrated in each home? Is it a separate area?

Peter: Yeah, so one thing we're really mindful here is we try to be actually only in luxury buildings that are in San Francisco which often build in coworking spaces in external common areas. They're also integrated within the building. And a big part of that is that we don't wanna be adding to the pressure of the rent-controlled market here, but so our common spaces here are more for hanging out. The coworking stuff tends to be the common areas out in the buildings or really there's just lots of great coffee shops everybody works in here, so that's where you'll find me most of my time. Every two hours I move to a new coffee shop.

Christine: Oh nice! And then are you in one of your homes right now? Where are you at right now?

Peter: Yes I am, actually. Right now I actually have a resident artist living here. He's actually a native San Franciscan and speaking to demographics, he's in his 70s, so he is using this home as basically his art salon to show his work. We're in a district called Dogpatch. Apparently he's in the art scene more than I am, but apparently there's a lot of things going on around here, but a block from us is something called the Minnesota Street Art Project, which is basically the art scene center of San Francisco, so with this home, we're trying to bring those artists in. We're giving subsidized memberships to two artists. Then with him and then also having the techies here so that they can meet and learn from each other and kind of create experience around that in this home. I haven't asked him specifically, but through my own analysis, he's about 70, yeah.

Christine: So what is your range or what's your average age of a person there? Does it just like go the spectrum?

Peter: It has really gone the spectrum, so in the last year and a half, again, like it started in probably more of the techie type and we had a hard time getting women in, let's say, whereas actually about two months ago I had home that was all women. But again, it's trying to push towards that access of changing that demographic, so we haven't been steady at any one per se. I would say we're really mixed. Average age right now is maybe, let's say 30, but yeah, we've got anywhere from 20 to yeah, up to 70. In the home I'm in right now, I would say actually the average age of all of that is maybe 45. The youngest being 35, so.

Christine: Cool. And then where do you see the future or what's your plan for the future of Haas?

Peter: Yeah, for sure. So right now, I think over the next year, it's really gonna be taking all the learnings I've gotten over the last year and a half and the team that I have helping me run everything and really solidifying these homes. Ironing out the kinks that we have definitely experienced over time. My view with technology and with many things is technology isn't really a threat, but I think a lot of people think it is. It's a way to free up people to focus on really human intrinsic activities, so I'm going to be using the next year myself, hopefully in the background. I keep quite busy in the front end too. Building up the systems to allow people to not be spending time in spreadsheets and tracking and doing stuff like that and just focus on hanging out and having fun with members, so the next year's probably going to be mostly doing that through these three homes, but long-term, what I'm trying to really create is a platform. I call it a digital living platform that enables people to kind of spin up these homes, not be locked down to the physical space, but I'd like to grow across San Francisco. I wanna have a home back in Canada. I'm living back there at times now, so hopefully in the next year opening a home there as well. One in Calgary and one in Vancouver. But, long-term, yeah again the idea is that you become a member and now you've got access to a home wherever you are. And the home being more than the physical space. So that's the big vision.

Christine: And then I know you guys are listed on coliving.com and I had Daniel Beck already on for an interview. He's amazing. So what software? I just would love a really clean directory. I know he's handling the booking, but it's just like this directory that links all of them together. Do you know of anything like that or can you develop it?

Peter: I would probably not be the right developer to do it. I'm more from the product management so I'm around ideas and building capacity some but I know what you're looking for, so I think Daniel is probably got the best thing out there right now. There's Nomad List which I'm assuming you're familiar with.

Christine: I love Nomad List. That's what I would model, I think would be perfect for coliving.

Peter: Exactly, exactly. So I think that Daniel's probably the closest to anything that's really gluing us all together so far, but yeah Nomad List, I would agree with you. And there's a lot of overlap there between what we're doing and the digital nomad movement, so yeah, those two would be the best resources right now for sure.

Christine: Cool. I'm connected to so many different ones, I might just have my developer do like a super simple directory where you just click and learn more. I'm sure one day somebody will develop it. I know Daniel's worked years on his and we use it also for the LA property. And then last question is the big one. Where do you see, Peter, the future of coliving in general?

Peter: I definitely think it's gonna continue to grow, I think that we've already seen this. Like even with companies like Airbnb, you know that's kind of a precursor to making this, normalizing this to be honest. San Francisco, when I came five years ago, anywhere else I lived, like the normal average parts of the world, like there was nobody I knew that would at all consider doing Airbnb whereas now, everybody's doing it. I think that coliving is kind of the first, front of the wave. I think without something of Airbnb or even the WeWorks of the world, we probably wouldn't have had the chance to drive this towards being more mass option, but I think that it is gonna become more normal. There's some videos out there that mock us, how we just invented roommates, but I think that coliving becomes what roommates is now, as everybody becomes more into this mindset. So it's about sharing connection versus transactional. Are you gonna pay this portion of the utilities kind of thing. I think it's got a huge potential. I think that it honestly is a grassroots movement. In my mindset, what I'd like to see it be, it can solve a lot of the social challenges we have in this world. If we're all more connected and understanding of each other. A lot of the things that we're suffering through right now kind of go away, because people maybe start helping each other overcome some of those challenges and I don't know, to me what's the point of living, having money if you don't have great relationships in your life. So and I think this is a way to help a lot of people find that because their social, cultural construct right now, I think prevents a lot of us from getting what we need from each other.

Christine: Oh and on that note, what a perfect ending, Peter. Thank you so much. We will definitely have all your contact information listed for Haas and if anybody's in San Francisco to look you up. And thank you again for doing this interview, I really appreciate it.

……….

Website: haascoliving.com

Interview with Jeffrey Sweetbaum | Cofounder of Playworking in Djurasevici, Montenegro

Christine: Okay, I have Jeffrey here. He is the cofounder of Playworking, which we're excited to hear about, over in Europe. You're originally from New York, right?

Jeffrey: I am in fact. But I've lived in Europe since 1990. I left the States a long time ago.

Christine: Well, we would love to learn more and hear more about Playworking, about your concept out there. Go ahead and tell us when you started, what you guys are all about. We'd love to hear it.

Jeffrey: Playworking started two years ago. Basically it's in a space which I had bought. I had intended it to house our guests in the summer. I have an adventure sports business here in Montenegro, which is an up-and-coming tourist destination for people from Europe. Cruise ships stop here a lot. I read about the whole movement and I just thought it was perfect for us, for Montenegro to set up a coliving space, particularly to attract people here in the off seasons. In the wintertime and in the spring. It's worked out well because we have really plenty of space during those periods of time. We have a very mild winter, so it's worked out well.

Christine: Perfect. How many people can stay in your concept at a time?

Jeffrey: Well, we have six on-suite rooms. Most people come in singles. On average, we have three people, four people at any given time. The tagline is, "Do deep work, then play." People really do do work here. It's hard sometimes to get them to go out and do the stuff that we can do with them because people are really coming here to do work, to catch up with work, to work on dissertations or they've got very specific job times they need to be online.

Christine: Then there's more of the work aspect in that home versus the play, you think?

Jeffrey: Yeah. What we try to do and what we hope to do is to help people create a fitness regime. The people that do that normally fit that into their regime easily, but the people who aren't used to doing it, it takes them a bit longer to get going. That said, a lot of people have done a lot more activities here than perhaps they expected and it's immediately available right out the door. We really do promote it. We do it ourselves. We've got a lot of stuff going on that people can join into when they want to. I guess everybody's just really busy nowadays. It's hard to get them to break away sometimes in the midst of a day or in the midst of a work period to go and do something. You have to try and set them up for it when they're able to do it.

Christine: And what's the average stay? How long do they stay on average?

Jeffrey: About a month. From a week to a month. I've had people here for longer. Very rarely, people shoot through for a few days. They're coming through the area and they need to just do something. They sit here and just really work all day. In general, people are here for two to three weeks I would say and maybe up to a month is close to average, but typically in the summer now.

Christine: Do you live there at the property also or do you live off-site?

Jeffrey: I live on the property. Since I've built it. Yeah.

Christine: Perfect. Then how active are you in the day-to-day? Is this a full-time business for you? Is it part-time?

Jeffrey: I'm also a serial entrepreneur. I have another business that's a startup that I'm working on and I have this adventure sports business here in Montenegro, which, It's seven years old. I'm out early in the mornings and then I get back in the afternoons. I do interact with people. I actually try and spend time with everybody and understand what they're here and what they're doing. That does happen. There is a lot more socialization. What I've realized about it is that people are looking for the social aspect. There is that. People who are here often get together, often go out together and often do stuff and go places. That's really cool. It's nice being part of it and it's nice fostering these friendships. People sometimes come here. They meet each other here and then they go off somewhere together afterwards. They go to their next destination together. They do keep in touch. I have people who knew each other and came here and were surprised to find each other here.

Christine: Oh, that's neat. I've heard that same story from other owners of coliving homes, where they meet at their home as strangers and then they start traveling the world together. That's cool. What is your average age of the people that stay there?

Jeffrey: I would say 30, maybe. A lot of people in their 20s and a lot of people in their early 30s.

Christine: Then do you guys host any events?

Jeffrey: What we do is we host activities. We host outings. We host tours to places and excursions to places. That we do on a weekly basis. People will go out with us two or three times during their stay at least. That's what we do.

Christine: What's the future growth plan for your concept for Playworking?

Jeffrey: Well, I think that really there's a house that's near us that's potentially available to remodel and to develop and add rooms. I'm thinking about that. It's also probably interesting to go closer to one of the towns here on the coast and look for space and look to build something with 20 rooms because. There are organizations that are bringing people from place to place. We might be able to facilitate that as Playworking and bring to bear all of the assets that we have to a different location in this region. Immediately, I would probably like to just build a few more rooms right nearby because we are getting more and more people here. We're full right now. We'll be full through September, pretty much.

Christine: Nice. Then my last question, the most important question, is where do you see the whole industry of coliving going in the future?

Jeffrey: Well, I guess I think it fits into a lot of people's futures, whether it's for a year or two years or three years. I'm not sure. I know it's possible to get tired of this lifestyle. I think a lot of people have already mentioned to me in their travels that it does get tiring after a while, but I think more and more people are able to do it. I guess everybody would like to do it at some point, so it's going to grow. It's going to grow and in a really good way.

....

Website: playworking.me

Interview with Eduardo Diego Herrero | Cofounder of Sun and Co. in Spain

Christine: Hello, I am here with Eduardo. He is the cofounder of Sun and Co., which is coliving in Spain. You're pretty close to Ibiza, right?

Eduardo: We're pretty close to Ibiza, yeah. I mean, for reference for those people who may not know Spain, or maybe they just know the main cities, we are on the Eastern coast of Spain, by the sea, in the Mediterranean, in a small town called Xàbia, which is south from Barcelona and south from Valencia, exactly like you said, in front of Ibiza.

Christine: Okay, so go ahead and tell us more about how you got started with Sun and Co., how long you guys been in business, and what you're all about.

Eduardo: We've been open for three years, almost three years now. We'll celebrate our third anniversary in September, September-October. The building where Sun and Co. is located used to belong to my family, to my grandparents, who were farmers there. It had been empty for quite a long time, so me and my cofounder, we decided to do something different, something that was interesting to us, which was to bring a little bit the concept of coworking a little bit further, and also make something related with remote work and digital nomadism. So we turned the building into what it is now, which is basically a community, building turned into a community for remote workers.

Christine: They work there, and can they also sleep there?

Eduardo: Yes. That's one of the things I think make Sun and Co. maybe a little bit different from other coliving concepts, which is that everything happens under the same roof. So basically, the whole ground floor are common areas and coworking space, and the first and the second floor are more private spaces, which are bedrooms.

Christine: Nice, okay. Then I also saw, when I took a look at your website, that you guys do kind of retreats for digital nomads. You guys do courses, classes, correct?

Eduardo: Yeah. We found that in the world, there are two big groups of coliving concepts. One are more maybe residential, such as Nest or such as Common or such as Outpost maybe, where others are more, we think, destinational. You are not exactly looking for a solution to your accommodation, and that's what we provide. People don't know exactly what they have never heard of our town before. They don't come because of the town. They come because of what we offer, the community and the activities and so on. These retreats and these courses and these workshops are one of the reasons why, well, people come to our place. We have a lot of people who come to work in the projects, but also for a specific retreat or workshop that we are organizing.

Christine: It looks like you cater more towards digital nomads, entrepreneurs, people that can work remotely. That's your main tenant or resident?

Eduardo: Yes. That's actually a requirement for us. You need to be working on a project. It doesn't have to be necessarily a digital project. We've also had, I don't know, PhD students or writers looking for a place where they can continue working while living abroad and while exploring other parts of the world, but we don't have, so to say, just local or just international tenants who want to stay in our place. They have to be working on something. That's also one little thing that maybe is different from other coliving spaces.

Christine: Perfect. How many people can sleep or stay at your property at a time?

Eduardo: Our maximum capacity is 20 people. It's kind of a medium-sized space. Well, it's small compared to city sizes, but it's proportional to the town size as well. After three years running the business, we've sort of discovered that around 20 people is the maximum amount of people that you can get to have a community feeling. We have the impression because we've also hosted bigger retreats, company retreats and bigger groups, that when you have 50 people, 70 people, the tendency is that the groups be by themselves. They split into two or three. With 20 people, I think we achieve that there is this family feeling that not everyone mingles or hangs out with everyone, but it's one feeling, one group. We think that's nice.

Christine: That's great. What's the average stay, typically?

Eduardo: That's a good question. It's kind of irregular. Our average stay is three weeks, four weeks. That's the time that people come to work with us and maybe because they want a break from routine. Maybe they just want to, I don't know, make a little escape from their cities or something. It's kind of irregular. Our average is three, four weeks, but we have staying one week. Then we have people staying three months. Most of them, they come to Europe. And for visa reasons, they are allowed to stay three months. They spend those three months with us. Although the average is about a month, we have very different streams.

Christine: Nice, that's what it sounds like. How often do you guys do events? If you do, do you guys invite the outside people into the events?

Eduardo: We have events almost every day, depending on the occupancy. The more people we have, the more events that we organize, and the more events our guests organize for the whole house, for the whole community. But we end up having them almost every day. They are sort of mixed. They're usually organized by people in the house, for people in the house, but we are starting more and more to open towards the local community and inviting people from outside of the house into our community. It changes a lot. It's also true that a lot of our activities are, so to say, non-specific for entrepreneurs. We also organize basically everything that the guests want to do. We ask them very often what their interest has, what they're looking for, what do you like to learn. We try to organize that for them.

Christine: Nice. Then, For Sun and Co., what is the future? What do you guys have planned? Any expansion plans?

Eduardo: Probably we're going to grow in number of beds in terms of accommodation. That's probably what we're going to do next year. Then we will continue working in the workshops, organizing events, other paid events for groups to come to our space and learn something. We try to focus on digital skills to give people skills to become digital nomads to be able to discover that they can have a job which is 100% remote.

Christine: That's definitely the way the world's going. We all know it. Always my final question is: Where do you see the entire industry of coliving, where do you see the future for coliving?

Eduardo: I think it's going to turning to a more professional industry. There are big startups in cities, especially American cities making big developments. The rest of the coliving initiatives are rather small, rather independent, such as ours. I think all of them are going to turn more professional. They are going to discover that they are in the hospitality industry. I think the hospitality industry is going to enter into the coliving concept a lot with a lot of money and also making big investments. So I think we'll see in the next years how everything changes a lot. Digital nomadism is also going to be much more mainstream, and remote work is going to be more normal. There will be more people traveling the world while they work, looking for communities. In general terms, it's going to grow. We also think that we'll see hotel chains blending into this world and doing whatever they think coliving is. Also Airbnb, probably.

Christine: Most definitely. Eduardo, thank you so much for your time today. I really appreciate it. This is awesome. If you guys are ever in Spain, go visit their property over there. I'm sure it's beautiful. Thank you again. Have a great rest of your day.

....

Website: sun-and-co.com

Interview with Stephen "Pip" Pippard | Founder and CEO of Pollen in London

Christine: Well, I'm excited because today I have Pip over in London with Pollen Coliving. He's going to tell us first about this beautiful artwork that he has behind him. This has got to be the best background so far.

Pip: Yes. When we tried to develop our brand, we wanted just not to have a vanilla. We wanted to have plain backgrounds and to inspire people by using local art, local issues, so we use recycled woods from film and TV sets and be commissioned. And Nathan who's a local street artist and now we're putting his art in all of our houses.

Christine: That's great. Launch into telling us when you started your coliving business, how many locations you guys have, all that fun stuff.

Pip: We started the research into coliving probably beginning of 2016. Launched our first building. Well, we've acquired our first building in October 2016 and launched it after a backs brick refurbishment in April 2017. We've now acquired four buildings, 25 rooms, and they're aimed to grown one new building about every three months.

Christine: Oh, wow. You guys have a good growth plan. That's awesome. Talk a little bit about to those that are watching that aren't familiar with London's real estate market, how hard is it for somebody to rent? I know you guys definitely have some sort of housing limitation.

Pip: To put it in the economics, if a young graduate comes out of college university, they're typically going to be on a starting salary of 25,000, maybe 30,000 a year and a typical, I don't know, one bedroom, two bedroom apartment in the areas that we operate in are maybe 3, 400,000... so it's 10 to 12 times the salary minimum. And since the crash in the financial back in 2008, banks, if you want to go through a mortgage, they typically want 10, 20% deposits. You'd have to come up with 40, 50,000 worth of cash, so it just puts that purchase beyond an awful lot of first time buyers now.

Christine: Oh, wow. Obviously your solution helps with that, right?

Pip: Yeah, yeah. Well, our typical housemate is 22 to 35. All professionals. We don't have students. We're trying to make our model specifically for young professionals and to singles. We don't have couples just because it affects the dynamic of the house, but that's something in the future that we want to do. We want to go for bigger premises and have maybe couples-only housing.

Christine: And we are the exact same. I agree 110% with that. It would shift the dynamics, so we're the same and it would need to be a separate house for couples, because we do have couples approach us. We want to do it, but yeah, I agree with you on that for sure. Pip, do you personally live in one of your concepts?

Pip: No, I don't. I keep them all within a, what 15, 20 minute drive away from my home. I'm hands-on. I do the management. I do the development. To give you a bit of background, I started in commercial property 25 years ago. I launched the second biggest service office provided to Regis back in '99. My background is service offices, so we've taken the concept of that flexibility from the office and commercial real estate together with some hotel background that I had and I'm trying to take the best parts and bring it in to residential property.

Christine: Have you been up against any challenges or any difficulties in industry?

Pip: Yeah, constructors, I guess, the construction teams. Trying to get them to understand the concept and try not to cut corners and we are a very high end boutique coliving concept, so we put in lots and lots of acoustic control, high end facilities, high end fixtures and fittings. When we approach our contractors, often they're not used to that high end within the shared accommodation, so it's trying to educate them and we've had to go through a couple of construction teams to get the right team to partner with.

Christine: Perfect. How many people per room in yours?

Pip: We have single occupancy rooms. About UK planning, what we call coliving in the UK is determined as houses of multiple occupation. I don't know if you've heard that phrase. Yeah, so there's legislation behind it in the UK. They're called HMOs and typically they work by greedy landlords trying to overpopulate small housing. Very similar to probably 20 years ago to this service office industry that was associated by fly-by-night type companies, so we've got a lot to prove to our neighbors, to the local community that what we're providing is actually something that is being demanded by the millennials, if you like, because they can't get on the property like the local residents did 10, 15, 20 years ago. We've got a bit of our PR within our local community, but once they see what we've done, how our housemates live and commute and the community we build, they're very happy with what we're doing.

Christine: Oh, good. No, that's interesting. I didn't know you guys had that legislation behind it. You're saying the workaround or what helps you guys differentiate between that? You said they have to have separate occupations?

Pip: No, you're limited to what you can or can't do. What we tend to do is the smaller house up to six occupants and you can do without going the formal planning route. We can do what we call the committed development rights, so that allows us to build, refurbish a building and have that ready within maybe three to six months. If we want larger occupancy, then we have to go down a planning route which could take six months. Our first one was a six. Our second one was eight which had to go to planning, an eight bed. Our next was seven and then we've gone for another six because we can do the churn quickly, but the larger, such as shared accommodation where we're talking, anything over seven occupants in a building has to go down this planning route.

Christine: Got it. Okay. That totally makes sense for sure. What's the average stay? How long do people typically stay there?

Pip: Ours typically stay about nine to 12 months.

Christine: Oh, nice. Do you have a minimum? Do they need to stay a minimum three months or something?

Pip: Yeah, we say three months minimum. However, the legislation the in the UK, again, on tenancy rights allows a tenant to be there for a minimum of six months, so once we get into a lease, then the tenant has the right to stay there for six months, so most of our tenants are there for a minimum six months.

Christine: Then do you guys host any events?

Pip: Yeah, we tend to try and do that once a quarter, so once we've got the house full, first thing we do is as we're filling with occupancy, we're introducing the housemates to one another, so trying to get them to socialize and we have lots of communal space for that to happen, but until we put an event together, it doesn't really gel the household, so we tend to have a pizza night and a film night and just try and get the housemates. We fund it. We order the takeaways, get the wine and the beer flowing, and just allow them to relax and get to know one another.

Christine: You guys do them quarterly, roughly? Oh, nice. Perfect. Then, what's the future for your coliving business over there at Pollen?

Pip: Well, personally, I want to sort of commercialize it more. There's some of the bigger players in the UK now. We've got WeLive due to move over here to jump over the pond. We've got The Collective which is the biggest coliving in the UK. I'm not sure if it's the biggest in the world, at the moment.

Christine: Rez Merchant, I'm hoping to interview him soon, he's jumping over to the US, so the opposite of what WeLive's doing, right? But we he's doing over there is amazing. I've watched interviews with him and his is huge. Have you visited any of his properties yet?

Pip: No, I haven't. I've done the video tours in various bits and pieces. I've been busy doing my own and I want not to be influenced by others, as well. Because I've come from a commercial service office background, I want to use my knowledge real estate, really, to make a USP and to differentiate from other providers, and so we want to stay boutique. We want to stay small in terms of the number of housemates in any one building. One will, say, move away from being in a shared house as a student. But our housemates are dictating that they don't want to live with more than maybe six or eight people.

Christine: And I agree, I'm the same. People will ask me if you know this one. I don't do a lot of research until my idea's kind of solidified and then I'll start looking at other things, and actually it's funny. That's where I'm at today. I have a WeWork location in Los Angeles that I work out of aside from working from my coworking space at home. I can't work there full time, so this kind of breaks it up, but it's exciting to see the growth. The faster everybody grows in the market, the easier it will be for us with smaller boutique concepts to be understood. When we say the world coliving, even in the States, still, it's like, "What does that mean?" It hasn't caught on yet.

Pip: Yeah, it's in education, but I was used to that 20 years ago. WeWork, we just brought that flexibility in workspace and there's a revolution now. I keep calling it the revolution in living accommodation and coliving is that. We've got a younger generation that don't accumulate stuff anymore. Everything is in the cloud. I've got a San Francisco-based tech business I'm housing in 50000 square feet in central London and you look at their staff. They're digital nomads. They carry everything in a backpack, pretty much. They want to experience stuff. They don't want to collect stuff and so they want that flexibility and ability to move at the drop of a hat to a certain extent.

Christine: Well, kudos to you for fully understanding that, right? And knowing the different generations. Again, I'm on the cusp of the millennial generation. I'm probably out of it, technically, but just having that understanding of how they wanna live and then catering to that is huge that you know to do that, and you're exactly right and our residents, same thing. They literally show up with a suitcase and a backpack and that is their entire life and these guys that are 28 to 31 years old, that's all they know. They want to experience it. They're traveling the world. They'll stay with us for a month and then they'll jump over to Europe and yeah, it's definitely changing, and I think it's good that we're all trying to build businesses that will cater to that, right?

Pip: Yeah, I think. I've been in property for a long time and when I left college, it was the first thing that your employee did was go get a mortgage, get those handcuffs so they can keep you to wage slave, and it's a different type of, I guess, how people live and their work/life balance is completely different, so how it was 10, 15 years ago... Apple produced the iPhone.

<u>Christine</u>: Now everything's at our fingertips. Anything is at a push of a button and I think people are used to that. Now they're calling it kind of like SaaS, Software as a Service, and now they're calling that HaaS which is Housing as a Service, and do you feel this way that it's shifting to actually providing a service?

Pip: We provide cleaning for our whole house for individual rooms and we're providing the broadband. Everything is just one built for housemates, so they don't need to worry about anything. They can go and get their food and they don't need to worry. It's a monthly fee that covers everything. There's other operators that will nickel and dime to try and get extra revenues. We're not interested in additional revenue streams. We want to minimize our void period as everyone does who owns real estate, but we're trying to build communities and if we have massive churn of our housemates, then that community spirit is not gonna build and evolve. We've got four houses now. We've only lost two housemates in the last 18 months. One moved in with his girlfriend, and a young lady had some family issues and needed to look after her younger siblings. They still come back to the house and have parties and meet up with the residents, so we're fulfilling on our ideals of trying to build that community.

<u>Christine</u>: With the four properties, do you guys have software that you're using to manage all of this on the backend?

Pip: We do. Yeah, and there's a couple of different things in the UK. They're financial software for the financial side of things and there's a system called Author. I don't know if it's over in the US. It can do everything. Sort of highlights all your maintenance issues and tells us about tenancy or your health and safety, sort of fire regulations, so you can put everything in there. We put tenants/housemates' birthdays in so we know when it's their birthday. We drop in, give them a card, and a bottle of fizz to go and celebrate with the rest of the house. It's called Author. It's been developing for a while. It can be integrated to a financial package where everything can be done, again, on the phone and while you're out and about, so in terms of invoices, everything can be all manually done while you're on the go which is, to be honest, a God send for me because as I've got three building projects on the go at the moment, I'm running from one building site to another as well as some of my commercial clients in the city, so I can manage my business literally on the phone.

<u>Christine</u>: That is great. Well, it sounds like there's exciting stuff coming up for you guys and for the history of coliving in general, so Pip, I appreciate your time on this interview. Thank you so much.

………..

Website: pollen.london

Interview with Rob Birch | COO of Gravity Coliving in London

Christine: Thank you so much, Rob. It will definitely be a lively conversation. I've actually been following Rob a little bit. We're all in the same message board over in Facebook for coliving founders. He asked a great question about what management technology is everybody using to manage their coliving homes, whether that be for bookings, community, etc. Are you guys able to narrow that down yet?

Rob: If I'm being totally honest, there's no perfect system out there at the moment, which covers coliving. Basically, because coliving is a mixture of hospitality, residential, events, and so forth, there's not one system that really brings all that together. So, it's quite an interesting topic where there's lots of potential for such a system to be created. At the moment, you can use bits of different software, but to actually merge it all into one space would be fantastic.

Christine: Oh, most definitely. I know that you're the COO and then there's actually two founders of Gravity. Can you tell us about Gravity, how you got started, when you guys are launching? All that fun stuff.

Rob: Yeah. So, basically, Gravity got started, because the two founders and myself, we've all seen the benefits and the drawbacks of relocating for work and we understand that it can really improve your personal and professional lives if you're in the correct environment. However, so many times, finding the correct environment is so difficult. So, we basically concluded that coliving is the answer to relocating and the new, global, working environment, so to speak. If you looked at the work environment with coworking, there's so many of these popping up now for the digital nomads of the world, but the residential market has been very slow to make progress into creating the environments and the properties that the new young professional and the new generations are really looking for. So, Gravity, we want to be the, kind of, much-needed catalyst that helps change the way that young professionals live, work and engage, within major cities and hubs around the world. The company got started around one year ago and we didn't want to rush into actually operating the properties straightaway. We wanted to do our research to really understand the potential that coliving has, looking at different locations, really streamlining our business model and, most importantly, looking to develop the tech platforms that we will need to create the perfect community and coliving space that we dream of having. And, at the moment, we are looking at three different locations, London, Barcelona, and Milan. And we're hoping to launch within the next six months.

Christine: Awesome. And then, will you, personally, live in any of the concepts or is it depending on where you launch?

Rob: I will definitely be living within one of the properties. I believe it's very important to actually see what it's like from a member, as well as from a working perspective. Also, my background in hospitality. I've helped run and grow hostel chains throughout Europe and what we found was, having people living on-site really helps, kind of, get over that barrier between staff and guests. And, I think it's an easier way to, kind of, get the community to work as one, because we don't want to have two separate people. We want to have everyone together. And we really want the community to help work with us, so to speak, and for us to help the community. Also, we'd love to have ambassadors living on-site, which may be anything from yoga instructors to website designers, social media people to, really, kind of, be the heart and soul of our community and make it a lot easier for people to transition into Gravity.

Christine: Love hearing that. And, I know we chatted, right before we started the recording, a bit about the largest coliving over there in London, which is the Collective. So, you've had experience. Have you visited their properties or do you know much about them?

Rob: Yes, I visited the property. It's a fantastic property. It's very large. From a lot of research, a lot of people are saying that the larger properties can be quite difficult to create the community, but at the Collective, they do a fantastic job with the different spaces they have from food and beverage spaces to well-being spaces, coworking, cinema rooms, gyms, etc. but they really help create a community of a mass size and it's very needed in London. London's one of the cities where you meet people every day, but you never actually have that meaningful engagement. And companies like the Collective and hopefully, Gravity, very soon, are helping make these connections actually happen and improve people's personal lives.

Christine: I love it. And then, what demographic are you guys going after? What age, male, female...

Rob: So, we're open to anyone and everyone. The most important thing for us is that they are open to the idea of community, collaboration and being themselves, but also being open to gain the wisdom from everyone else around them. We really want it to be that hub. We're not looking for students. Master's and PhD students potentially, but we're looking for the young professionals. People who are looking to really go somewhere with their lives. And, I'd say, between the ages of around 22 to 35 would be the average, male and female. We're open to everyone.

Christine: Perfect. That seems to be the common demographic across the board, so that's perfect. I've got some additional questions here. How often would you guys have or are you guys planning on hosting events and will you invite outside people to the events?

Rob: Good question. So, we'll be hosting events and activities and also services throughout the week. We'd love to have at least one event, or one activity, every day of the week. These will be based over three of our community pillars. Either personal well-being and group well-being, professional growth and also meaningful engagement. So, going through the personal well-being, this could be things like, morning yoga, nutrition classes, group counseling about stresses at work, etc. as well as, professional growth. So, things like social media marketing to website design, to group talks, meetups and industry-specific talks from experts from around the city. Then, the meaningful engagement. That's where we want to work with local companies and global companies, bringing in their products and their services and creating events where people can relax and actually engage with people on a higher level than you do just bumping into them on the street, so to speak. We don't want to be a world community. We want to really help our members, kind of, grow into the wider community around. A lot of our target people will be people relocating and it may be a new language, a new city, a new environment all together. So, we want to help them get within the local community and be able to be themselves in that community, whilst also helping grow the local community outside. So, it would definitely be open to everyone and some of them will be free. We'll also have more of the premium services, activities, and events, which will be at the cost, but we want to be open to everyone and we really want to create a community that means something.

Christine: I love hearing that. So then, my last question is, looking at the big picture, where do you see the future of coliving?

Rob: So, to start with, a lot of people say coliving is a new movement, when, the way I look at it, coliving has been around from the tribal times to where I'm from, in the South Wales Valleys, with the mining communities. People have always lived together and have helped people and helped each other. I think, in recent years, coliving has turned to cities mainly and I see coliving being the future of housing policy. I think it really helps, both the issues of densely-populated cities, helping personal issues like depression. And I really see there'll be coliving villages, coliving nurseries, coliving nursing homes, and coliving for families. I really see it as being the way forward. The more connected we are, the better we are as a human race, in general. So, I think there's a big future for coliving. I think this is just the beginning of a whole new chapter and it's good to be involved in it.

Christine: That was the perfect soundbite on coliving. You're exactly right. I agree 110% about the importance of community. And I think people are figuring that out now, finally. We had a little stint there where everybody was kind of isolated, but hopefully that's shifting. Well, Rob, thank you so much. I can't wait to see your guys' future growth. It's going to be so fun to watch.

....

Website: gravitycoliving.com

Interview with Eric Yang | Founder of Influencer Summit

Christine: Okay, you guys, I am really excited because we are actually here with Eric Yang, who is actually he's in Paris, France right now, as we speak. I wanted to do these interviews with experienced people that are living this lifestyle already, and have for a few years. Eric's going to go into his story. So, he doesn't run his own coliving home, but he's actually lived in them. He's a digital nomad. He's traveled the world. He actually lived in the original Epic Entrepreneur House with us, back maybe a year and a half ago. So much fun. I will let Eric go ahead and tell his amazing story, and his experiences with coliving and traveling the globe.

Eric: Hey, everybody, so my name is Eric Yang. I am 22 years old, and like Chris mentioned, I am in Paris right now, which is where I was born and raised. I have a lot of international background. My parents are Chinese; born in Paris. I moved for my last year of high school to China a full year, graduated there. I didn't know what I wanted to do after high school, so I took a gap year between high school and college. So I took my backpack and went to Argentina for six months to work in a daycare. I didn't know how to speak Spanish, I didn't know anybody there. I just went to a hostel and lived there for six months. That is when I first tasted like the digital nomad lifestyle. Where I didn't have an agenda, I didn't have a house. I didn't know anybody, but just loved the new adventure, right? It's like a new map, where just you going through the journey of discovering where you are, who you want to be friends with; I just loved it. I was sharing my room with six other people. It was in the middle of summer, so it was like really, really hot. I slept on the couch a couple of times in the living room, because it was like so steamy in the room, it was impossible, but I loved every single moment of it, because I was just free. After that, I went to the US, to college in the Santa Barbara, in the California. I was there for two years, and after graduating/dropping out of school. And I do this, because I told my parents I graduated, but not really. I dropped out. I took a gap year where I could focus on my business. Was like in an event for entrepreneurs for young hustlers and young leaders in LA, and because I wanted to travel even more, I took my online and I created online events where it allowed me to travel even more. So, I went to Bangkok after that, and I traveled in Southeast Asia. I built virtual summits, which was my main way to monetize and finance my travels. After a couple weeks, back in 2017, March, I move into the entrepreneur house, where Christine was living with us in San Diego. Honestly, I miss it so much. Ever since I left the house, and the people that was in it. It was just such a blast, and such a unique experience to be able to share this coworking, coliving experience with people you actually care about; who you actually look up to as well.

Christine: Nice. Oh, that's great. Since then, you jumped to Thailand, how many countries have you been to since?

Eric: Yeah. So, from high school till now, I think I've been to over 20 countries. My main way to travel is mostly like with a backpack. So, just put it like basic clothes. Like two or three pairs of pants, two or three t-shirts. You buy everything in the country you go to. One laptop, because you have to work; you cannot always have fun. Yeah, so the biggest and best country I've been a part of, where I actually lived long term, was San Diego, and Bangkok, by far.

Christine: Perfect. That's why I'm glad you're doing this interview and you can show the advantages and disadvantages and just why you chose that. Is it mostly the freedom? Of just not being attached to things?

Eric: Yeah. That, a lot. So, I never know what I'm going to do next. So, I don't like to have something forced upon me, like having a lease, for example. Like when I was in college, I didn't like the house I was living in, but I had a lease, so I had to stay there. Or I had to find someone else to take up my lease so I can leave and they take my spot. But when I travel, it's always like Airbnb, hostels, I Uber around, I don't have to drive a car. I don't even need to. It's like so convenient to Uber or take a taxi around the country you go to, especially in cheap countries. Just being able to just say tomorrow if I want to go to Japan, or tomorrow if I want to go to Chile, or Uganda, I can, because I have nothing. I have no rent, and I have no house. Yeah, just having this freedom, because I know that, eventually I will have to settle down somewhere, to have like a more stable environment to build a bigger business, or bigger personal environment where I can thrive. But for now, I just take full advantage of what's in front of me. So, this freedom is just what I needed. If I had a house or a car I wouldn't be able to do that.

Christine: No, that's true. Then so on the flip side, what are the things that are hardest about being like location independent and jumping around? What are like some of the hard parts?

Eric: Yeah. There were a lot of times where I was lonely. I felt like, I don't want to go out. Especially when I'm in a new country sometimes, like I'm tired of socializing around some people. I am personally, a social introvert. I like to be around people, but I recharge by being by myself. Sometimes, I want to recharge by being with other people that I only know a lot, and sometimes those people I know a lot, I don't have access to them. Next to me, because they are either working or they are not traveling with me. So definitely the people, my friends. Family is okay to be honest, I talk to them once in a while, on the phone, so like once a week, so that's fine. But the whole experience of being able to share this journey with real friends, right? Being able to look back 10 years from and not just strangers who met somewhere in the world, and being able to share this experience. So, that's like one, with friends. Two, building like a strong routine. So, as an entrepreneur, I love to have a schedule. Meaning, I love to wake up at 8am, get my coffee, do my workout, with my cool workout buddy. Which I had in San Diego, which was awesome. We just push each other with our diets. We had to eat 3600 calories every single day. And every single day we're like, hey did you eat your chicken yet? Or did you drink your pot of coffee, yet? And that was like the fun part, right? Like you're a cannonball with your roommate or with your friend, but when you travel, you're like all by yourself. So you have to rely on yourself a lot. Sometimes, I know I don't have the self-discipline to just push myself to do something, like I said routine over and over again, in a new environment, because you have to find a gym. You have to find a restaurant that fits your diet. Sometimes you have to travel a lot, so you're kind of tired, and your whole balanced schedule is all off. So, I really miss the ability to have the potential of the ability to do something over and over again. You know, just focus on the things I needed to get done, but when I travel it's really hard, and I have to comprise on other things.

Christine: The routine. And I've heard that too, a lot. Is that it's hard to have that solid routine when you have to get back into it, and sometimes it takes a week or two to get your routine down.

Eric: Hundred percent.

Christine: And something else I'll mention that's amazing about jumping around, is when I went to Paris back in December, Eric just happened to be there at the same exact time. Yeah, he got to show me around his city, it's really cool to forge these relationships, on like a global level, and stay connected through social media. I think social media is a great tool to keep the connection, but then to have that human component, and interaction is cool, too. So you've done hostels, you've done Airbnb, you've done actual coliving home. Because you were in our home for three months. Then what do you look for when you do to decide where you're going to stay? What do you look for?

Eric: Before it was how cheap it was. In Chiang Mai where I was like three months ago, I stayed in a hospital/hostel that costed me like one US dollar per night. So the reason why I call it a hospital is because I actually took massage classes. In Chiang Mai, massage classes are taught in hospitals. So, I stayed in a hospital where I had like a long tatami, where I was sleeping on with a fan on. In the morning I would go to the Thai massage school, and learn how to do Thai massages and the whole oil thing. I would sleep on a one dollar bed, because I was looking for backpacking experience. I did it for a week. Massage school was great. But now the thing I'm looking for is I changed my way of traveling, now I'm traveling more with friends because I want to share the experience of living with other people. Like living experiences; sharing the housing expense as well. So now it's like three or four bedrooms, so I can go with three or four of my buddies, when I go and travel around. Try, I try to replicate the entrepreneur house business model, through my traveling, by inviting friends to come over and we have like our work schedule, our work sessions, our work out, our diet. So that was great, but now it's like decent WiFi, like stable WiFi. A pool is always a bonus if you go to Southeast Asia when it gets really hot. Yeah, just good air conditioning, if there is any.

Christine: What a great story. That's awesome. And you're modest, you won't say, but Eric's come from a pretty privileged background. So be able to live in these third world countries and sleep on a cot for a dollar a night, that's really cool. That you want to experience life so much, that you're like hey, it's cool. I just want the adventure and to meet people. That's really neat.

Eric: Yeah. When I lived in the entrepreneur house in San Diego, the biggest perk of being part of the house is knowing that you are living with amazing people that you vibe with because everybody there has to be conscious minded, on top of being successful, and being conscious minded attracts other conscious minded people. So when you're friends with four people in the house, isn't like only four people, because those people have other friends, so without really meaning to, you have a big circle of friends with amazing talents. With amazing gifts. And you're able to just connect with them, because they're just good people. So, when you are in a coworking space, or coliving house, just being able to meet people so easily. Because I found it, personally, really hard to meet good people if you're outside of their inner circle, because you never know where are the good people, you never know who are the entrepreneurs in a foreign country because they speak a different language. I was really lucky in the first place that I got access to the network when I was in California, but when I went to Bangkok, it was really hard for me to find any good entrepreneur that I vibe with because one, I don't understand the language, or two, because I didn't know where to find them. So, just easy access is just so underrated.

Christine: Definitely. Tell the viewers how many languages, which languages do you speak? I think three, right?

Eric: So, I speak like three and a half. I speak French, English, and Chinese. I speak a bit of Spanish, because I lived in Argentina for a while, and I took Italian for four years in high school, but I forgot all of my Italian because I learned Spanish, and they're so similar. So I speak like a mixture between Italian and Spanish now, which is kind of weird. And all of that with a French/Chinese accent, which is even weirder.

Christine: That's awesome. I think that's amazing. Well, my last question for you, Eric, is in your personal opinion, and you're a smart guy obviously, where do you see the future of coliving and housing as a service? As like the new industry disruption. Where do you see that going?

Eric: So, I have two perspectives on that. One, as a young entrepreneur that is like part of the gen Z generation as well, and two from like a business perspective, because I actually work with one of our roommates on an Airbnb event. So I have a little bit of experience in this industry. So, talking about myself, personally, first is I don't want to be attached to anything right now. So when it comes to have any kind of engagement with or commitment, that's the word, commitment to any kind of physical possessions, like houses or cars, I don't need it, because when I travel I'm looking for experiences, not like material things. If I do, I can buy it or rent one. So, for now I think a lot of young people, they either don't have the money to have like long term lease, because they might have debt, they don't know where they're going to pay their rent next. Maybe going to a coliving space at a hostel is cheaper options for them, or going back to their parents if they need to. We don't have another legal need to pay for rent when they are not there anymore. Also, for the people who just want to be around entrepreneurs, or like when the people are around the same hobbies and passion are able to share an experience without getting attached to a specific location, for like a long time. When they can just jump around from one community to another, is truly underrated right now. Because from my perspective, once I got out of college it was like way, harder for me to socialize, because there wasn't like a place where I would go to every single day to meet the same people over and over again. I don't have a nine to five job, I don't have an office. I don't go to classes anymore, so my only way to meet people, is either like meetups or through friends of friends or on Tinder. Which is kind of great sometimes, when you travel. Which is a super underrated hack, if you want to meet local people. Even as friends, it's even great because even if you're interested in them like dating wise, by having a friend in the local place you're staying at, they can introduce you to their other circle, which is great. So you can have the full immersed experience, but I diverge here. Let's finish up with Airbnb really fast. Like, no more than ever, young people don't have the money to buy houses anymore, because one, houses are getting so much more expensive. They have to pay for college debt, if they have not. Inflation is jumping like crazy. Even if they are interested to buy a house, they'll still like pretty young, even if you're 27, 28 you don't know if you want to live in a certain city for long, because it changes so much, and because now, with jobs, anybody can get fired four years from now, because the jobs are getting replaced by other AI or cheap labor. So maybe their company's going to fire them, so they have to find a new job, and maybe their dream job, or a job where they would make enough money isn't in the city they are staying at. So they will have to go to another city, and rent a new place. So, you never know what the future is going to bring to you. So being able to adapt yourself to your environment is really important, so Airbnb is great for you if you want to go and stay in a place for short term, but I just want people to open their eyes to this new world of coliving, short term renting, not getting attached to any kind of big commitment anymore, because things change so fast. Just think about who you were like six months ago. You changed so much, did you expect where you would be today? Or where you be with like your business today? And if you had to travel to another country or another city? You never know what's going to happen, and being able to say, yes, much more easily is such a big freedom for us entrepreneur. Even if you're not, it's just such a gift for you to be able to go anywhere at any time.

Christine: Exactly. Perfect, Eric. We'll end on that note. Thank you so much for taking the time to do this interview. It was amazing. It gives our readers and our viewers a chance to hear somebody that actually does this and experiences this and what you guys look for. And again, it's the commonalities. It's like freedom, not being locked down, being able to jump wherever they want. You know, that's the way the world's going, so we're excited to push the concept even further. So, thank you so much, Eric.

Interview with Ken Conklin | CEO of Gravel to Castle

Christine: Okay, hello everybody, Christine here with Kindred Quarters. So excited today to have Ken Conklin, he is the founder/CEO of Gravel to Castle for premium branding. His work is impeccable. He has a rockstar team. So let's launch right into it, Ken. Talk about your journey. When did you get started? How did you do it? What made you do it? How often do you travel around?

Ken: Yeah, so I was 18. I went to a Catholic high school and everyone I went to school with were going to high end colleges, some in state. I was the one kid that went to this high school that realized, "You know what? I don't wanna do the traditional route. I want to do something different." So literally two days before I was supposed to go down to U of A in Tucson, Arizona, I decided to withdraw and try to figure out some other alternative to doing the traditional route. I had no game plan but I knew that i was making the right choice by not making the wrong choice. I worked for six months at a Subway. It sucked. All my friends were in college having the time of their life and here I was not progressing. So I had a really low point and, not a lot of family issues, but things that everyone deals with. I got to a point where I realized, "You know what? I have nothing to lose. Why don't I go chase my dreams?" So I literally moved to California with, I think, a thousand dollars and a camera. So enough to barely have one month's rent and that's it. I had to figure stuff out right away. So I moved to California, Santa Barbara, in January of 2016 and that was when I was like, "You know what? I'm going to go all in on creating content and creating things that people can watch and experience a certain emotion, or whatever, and story tell." So I moved there, I actually went to school for a little bit in Santa Barbara, and I just started taking photos every day. I had my lead job at Levi's and then I was creating content and doing some freelance stuff on the side, at the beach, downtown all the time. It got to a point where I got pretty good at creating content and doing social media stuff. That's when I actually kind of shifted directions and started doing marketing for this student housing company. It was awesome. It was the best job I could've ever had, especially being 19, being the marketing director, running around, filming apartment complexes and doing all this website stuff. It was amazing, but it got to a point where I realized, "You know what? I'm not fulfilled. I could be doing this for other people and have a bigger impact and everything." So that's when I literally booked a one-way ticket to Maui, Hawaii. I quit my job. I quit my school. Literally just packed up everything. The crazy thing is, I didn't know anyone in Hawaii. I literally had no game plan, but all of a sudden I had this sense, this urgency inside me saying, "I gotta go chase my dream right now." I literally just landed in Maui the next day at noon, opened up my laptop, looking on Craigslist for a place to stay. For two hours, it was very stressful because no one was getting back to me. I was calling people saying, "Hey, I see you have a room for rent. I'd love to come check it out." They'd be like, "Oh yeah, you can come check it out next Monday." In my head I'm like, "Uh, I need to do it now because I have no place to sleep." Fortunately I actually found an amazing place that night. It was the perfect place, right near the beach. It was an amazing house. That's kind of how I got myself into it, but I got to a problem where I realized that I didn't have like-minded people around me that could help me achieve all the things that I wanted to achieve. I actually moved to San Diego where there's a lot of entrepreneurs, that whole community where everyone's focused on living their dream and having fun, but also creating an impact and all the different areas that you wanna be well-balanced in. That's what's awesome about Kindred Quarters is literally you're living with other entrepreneurs that do the same thing. They're digital nomads, or location independent and whatever it is, but they also are focused on the same end goal that you have, which is on the big scale, create a big impact and live life on your own terms and all that stuff. It's cool because everyone has their own business. It's not the same business. They all have whatever businesses they run and so I feel like every Monday there's some masterminds, you get so much value from hearing other people's perspective when you're talking about your own business. What you're dealing with in terms of challenges for that week. All of a sudden you get outside perspectives that you wouldn't even think about because you're always stuck in your own head.

Christine: Yeah, and that's how I met Ken was that he stayed at the original Epic Entrepreneur House in San Diego for like two weeks. And it was just great having him in our home. It was just so much fun.

We had a blast creating content and I think you're exactly right, just being around like -minded people is huge. Since then, I know you've jumped around. Your longest stint was staying in San Diego, right? And then now, so in the last couple months tell people where you've kinda jumped around to.

Ken: So, I've been to Arizona, and actually the only two states are Arizona and California within the past two months. But, I've bounced around a lot because for me, my particular business, how I market myself is creating fun content that gives value to people and helps them with marketing and branding their business, but also gets people to go, "Wow! That's really cool watching." So I've just simply been from San Diego to Los Angeles, a lot of Hollywood area, to Santa Barbara to Phoenix, Scottsdale, Arizona. Bouncing around quite a bit because I don't like to stay in one place for too long. I think that's the millennial generation is, we're always so quick to bounce around from thing to thing. That's why you have to be careful with that because in the business world you wanna focus on one thing, right? You wanna focus on one thing and dominate it. Fortunately, I've been able to control that emotion for my business and stay in one lane and not bounce around. In terms of living and lifestyle, I always like to switch things up every couple weeks, for sure.

Christine: Yeah, and that was my next question, is it hard to keep a really solid routine when you're traveling and jumping around? Or are you pretty dialed in on your daily routine?

Ken: When it comes to getting work done, on the business, that's pretty dialed in because I keep a very tight schedule. I follow, basically, the schedule I create for myself the next day. That comes first before anything else. But, because I'm working on so many video projects, things have gotten not necessarily unorganized, but unstructured. It's definitely been a bit of a challenge, especially with working out and having a gym and knowing the area. When you're bouncing around from place to place, you definitely have to adjust and be able to adapt very quickly.

Christine: Adapting, that's a great word. So what's your favorite thing about your lifestyle and the way you live? And then what's the thing about it that you don't like?

Ken: Well the, I'd say the favorite thing is the unknowing. It's a constant adventure. I have a very positive attitude and I'm always down for some new experience. Definitely every single day is a new experience living this type of lifestyle and I like the idea of not having to be in a particular place at a certain time. That's how I structured my business. To make sure that the value I bring to my clients, I don't have to be in person. That's a big thing that I really focused on this past year, to make sure that I could have the luxury of being in a situation like that. Some of the downsides, if you're not around the like-minded people, that us entrepreneurs need to be around 24/7, then you can slip or fall off just a tad bit in some areas, because you don't have the constant push of different perspectives and everything. People saying things that are positive or all of a sudden sparks something inside you that you wouldn't even think about if you were just in your own head.

Christine: That's a great point. At least tell the funny story about last year in Los Angeles, how you booked on Airbnb. You have to tell that story.

Ken: Okay, so I always heard all these stories about people traveling the world and staying in hostels and how it's not too bad. I'm like, "okay, yeah." Everyone says you meet awesome people there, but they're always talking about being in Bali, or being in some other country. For some reason I was like, "You know what? Let me go try this in downtown Los Angeles." After that one night, I realized I never want to do that again. I was fine. I survived. I'm still here, but it was just a very awkward experience around people that aren't entrepreneurs or aren't doing the same thing as you. There could be potential problems if you're around people that you don't know and trust, and maybe they're going through whatever things in their life. I don't know, so let's just say I'm gonna make sure I don't ever do that again. That's why we need to make sure we have plenty of Kindred Quarters locations all over the place.

Christine: So that is a downside, right? You're not in this network. You guys are jumping around. You guys don't know people. That's been a common theme on these interviews as a downside to that lifestyle.

Ken: Because I experienced that, I know what I don't want. On structure, maybe you lose kinda routine, from bounce around from place to place, you certainly learn how to adapt much quicker versus simply not ever going through those experiences and then all of a sudden it happens at a time that you can't really afford to have it happen and then you fall off, or things really mess up. I definitely fortunate to have gone through all the experiences to learn, to grow, all those things.

Christine: So then, we already talked about how you do Airbnb. You do coliving. You've done hostels, now. What do you look for when you decide to stay at a place? I know you're very last minute. You just kinda jump around. And what is it that attracts you to that listing?

Ken: The biggest thing is, obviously I want to be in a nice place, but I want to also be around people, especially the right people. I'd say on a broad scale, it's being around other business owners, entrepreneurs, that way I know I'm around people that see the world the way I do where we can live and become whoever we wanna become. They're hard working. They chase their dreams. They also have a desire to have some sort of impact. Not just achieve their own success, but also somehow make the world a better place. That's one thing. To be more niched down, I would love to be around other content creators. My biggest focus right now in my business is really going all in on my personal brand creating video content, interviews, all these things that really push my message out to the world. If I could be around people that not only are the entrepreneurs that are hardworking, but also are doing the same thing, where we'd all be in the studio collaborating on an interview or giving value content. Stuff like that, that would be the most ideal thing for me, at this time, at least.

Christine: Do you go on Facebook and do you put it out to your network? Like, "Hey, I'm going to be in Los Angeles next week." and try to find that core group of people to find an Airbnb together with?

Ken: So, fortunately I'm able to post on Instagram stories and say, "Hey, I'll be in Los Angeles. Who's wants to link up?" Or whatever, and I'll have quite a number of people that respond to that, because I have decent following all throughout southern California. That's one way, but I don't really actually leverage to Facebook, because I have a ton of people in southern California that are just like us, so I probably should start levering that because I'm sure I could find some amazing, credible people that way. But, simply just Airbnb, the website, and I guess my network that I already know of and talk to on a daily basis. That's been my strategy so far.

Christine: And then what do you travel with? How much stuff do you travel with? Do you have suitcase and a backpack?

Ken: Oh, I am a minimalist, big time. I literally have my backpack which has my laptop, my camera, some equipment. That's what's nice about my business, is I don't need a whole lot. I also have my tripod, but I don't even use it that much because most of the time I'm creating cool stuff and traveling around versus being stable in place. Then I just have a big duffel bag that has my nice boots that I can either go to a club, or film, or be on video with. Simply some nice Nike shoes to go running or do whatever, and then flip flops. And then a couple other change of clothes. I have my suit, too, so it's like whatever outfit I need for whatever situation.

Christine: That is so awesome. I'm so intrigued by how everybody's just scaling down their lives to create more freedom.

Ken: That's what's awesome. Everyone's different. Everyone has their own points in their life, desires, but for me I'm not attached to any particular things at all. I have plenty of other nice suits, or any other shoes that would be nice to have all the time, but I would rather just have that in a storage unit so I can be traveling pretty light. That's why I just need my laptop. As long as I have my laptop, I'll stay sane. If I didn't have that then, no, I'd need all my stuff.

Christine: So yeah, laptop and a charger, that's all we need. Okay, so my last question for you is, in your personal opinion, where do you see the future of coliving and housing, providing housing as a service and making it more flexible?

Ken: Well, it's so interesting because, you know I was born in 1997, so I kinda grew up with these Gameboys and then the iPads and then the iPhones, and all these different things. This world, this new age of technology that many people didn't experience or grow up with if they weren't born in that era. So, it's been so normal to see all these services, like Uber, Airbnb, that are totally changing the game and totally transforming our day to day and how we operate. I think it's going to be a totally normal thing, especially with Kindred Quarters and this entrepreneur world, for people to have a desire to live with other like-minded people, instead of just being alone. This past year I lived in an awesome place that was by myself, and it was great but I got lonely. I wasn't around like-minded people 24/7 and so it's important that I am in that environment because without it you don't have the constant up-leveling that all the other people give you when you're around them.

Christine: Awesome, Ken! Well, thank you so much. This was an amazing interview. I really appreciate your time today. Where are you off to now? You're in west Hollywood now, right?

Ken: I'm in West Hollywood, currently. Probably in about 20 minutes I'm gonna head to Santa Barbara and collaborate with some other awesome people and film an awesome video project, so I'm excited for that.

Christine: Good stuff. Okay, well we will talk soon and again I appreciate it. Thank you so much. Have a great day!

Interview with Dan Schwartz | Founder and CEO of InvestorFuse

Dan has a passion for helping the overwhelmed real estate entrepreneur work smarter and earn more by setting up effective systems. After launching InvestorFuse, a lead management workspace for real estate investing, he's helped bring the power of automation to hundreds of happy investors and has built a strong community around the technology. When not working or investing, you'll find Dan traveling, drumming, or helping other entrepreneurs grow their businesses.

<u>Christine</u>: Hello everybody! Christine McDannell here with Kindred Quarters. I'm so excited to have Dan Schwartz on. He is the CEO of InvestorFuse and a dear friend of mine and was a roommate of mine in the Entourage House in San Diego for six months, so we know each other well. I was always envious of his stories of traveling the world for a whole year, right, as a digital nomad, like a year straight. Yeah, I will let Dan get right into it and tell his story. What's nice too, you guys, is some of these interviews are with guys that are in their early 20s. They said we're not going to go the college route. We're just going to travel, jump around, be a digital nomad. Now we have a few interviews coming up with guys in their early 30s, so you can see that it's not necessarily an age thing. I think it's just this sense of freedom that we want to have. Dan, go ahead and take the floor.

Dan: The endless summer, if you will. I'm driven a lot by freedom. It's built into the companies that I create and generally my lifestyle, especially location independence. I feel like the whole coliving movement speaks exactly to that sort of motivation. It's very fortunate to have met Christine when I did and meeting that whole crew of entrepreneurs in San Diego, which is a really tight-knit group of entrepreneurs at all live together and they colive, and it's an accountable system that really lets you step your game up while also giving you a built-in social network. It was huge for me, especially since I didn't really know anyone else in San Diego. It's one of the best life hacks of our modern generation, and it works regardless of age. I find that you could probably be 50 and still find a good coliving situation depending on your marital status. A quick background on my story. I've always sort of been a nomad. When I was in my early 20s, I was touring full-time in a band called Pigeons Playing Ping Pong. I played the drums. You can look them up. They're still around. I was always hopping around. I left the band when I was 26 or 27 because I wanted to have some of my 20s to myself, to explore the world and travel. What I did is I built a recurring revenue model business that allowed me to separate my income from my time and essentially just do what I want, hang out with people I want to hang out with, serve the people I want to serve, and travel and live wherever I wanted to. It came down to the point where if I could actually post up anywhere I want in the world, where is the most ideal location? I chose San Diego, and that's how I met Christine McDannell, and got introduced to the whole coliving entrepreneur house movement. I would say it was a life-changing experience for me.

Christine: Nice. I know you had a time where you lived in San Diego, what, for six months, you had your own loft in Little Italy?

Dan: Yeah. I started it by living on my own, but I found that I was just hanging out with all of the coliving people anyways, so eventually it made sense for us to find a really nice house where we could all split the cost and make it affordable and practical. We ended up moving into this baller house in San Diego with a pool and a hot tub and a sauna and a view of downtown San Diego. It was just an amazing, ideal six months. I'm sad that it didn't last longer than it did, but we had at least that cut off after six months. That was earlier this year, so I'm still grieving.

Christine: Yeah, me too. We all are. That was a cool house for sure. We still have videos and pictures to always relive the memories of the Entourage House. We've got some questions. How much stuff do you own right now?

Dan: I'm an essentialist or a minimalist, however you want to put it. I really only own things that I'm going to use. If I don't use it for more than 60 days, then I just leave it behind. I really only own clothes and a laptop and a toothbrush. Everywhere I go really over the last four years have been furnished units that didn't require any furniture or kitchenware or really anything. Really the only thing that I permanently own are a notebook, maybe some books that I'll travel with, my drumsticks and my clothes and my laptop. It's a super minimal lifestyle, but once you get used to that, you start to realize that maybe I don't need all of this other stuff that I don't actually use, but I feel like I'm attached to so I don't want to get rid of. I got rid of those attachments a long time ago, so I'm used to this minimal setup.

Christine: That's awesome. Well, your DJ equipment, didn't you leave that behind with a good friend?

Dan: Yeah. Hobby equipment is totally fine. I can justify that expense because it gives me joy and it's fun. When I'm traveling, I have to leave that kind of stuff behind. I have a keyboard and some beat-making devices, but I left that with our mutual friend in San Diego. I'll get back there at some point.

Christine: What's your favorite part about living this more free lifestyle?

Dan: I crave novelty a lot. Being location-independent and being able to operate your business virtually and having friends in different locations just makes for an interesting, fun and exciting life. You always have a trip to look forward to and you have to learn to enjoy the moment obviously, but there's always something to look forward to, and there's always something new to experience in different cultures and adventures that you can have. I think having the capacity to live a life of adventure is something that every human deserves. If you're limiting yourself from experiencing that then that's what ... It drives me to give more people that capacity. I'm thankful to come on and share this message on your interview here.

Christine: I appreciate it because you legitimately have traveled the world and lived a life, and you run a successful large company. What are the pros and cons to running a large organization? Again, you could run it virtually, which is great, but you have team members, you have staff. What are some of your hacks? Do you guys do weekly Zoom meetings?

Dan: Well, the bigger the company is, the less work you have to do. I should say the less busy work you have to do and the more focused work you have to do. Focus work doesn't necessarily mean eight-hour days or even five hour days. I only work really a couple of hours a day of focused planning with my team, thinking and strategy type of high level stuff, which doesn't require a lot of traditional busy work typing stuff on the computer. All my team is doing that, so it shifts your priorities around. I think of running a bigger team as a forcing function to become a better leader. When I have all this extra time because most of the monotonous work has been taken off my plate, it forces me to learn how to be a better leader, and it forces me how to be a transformational leader that can actually give people challenging and fun projects and problems to work on that actually help them grow as well. The bigger the company gets, your role as a leader changes a little bit. I'm going through that right now where we have a 15 or 16-person company, and I have to make sure that everybody is motivated all the time, which doesn't necessarily take up a lot of time, but it takes more focus and courageous effort on a day-to-day basis. That's what I've learned and that's the transition you'll go through as you scale a company like that. If it's just you, then you have to really challenge yourself on working on essential things that you actually enjoy doing and being ruthless about delegating the stuff that you hate to do or you're just not good at, and you'd be doing your company a disservice by doing the stuff that you're not good at. It's important to really get good at honing in on your unique skill sets and taking the leap of faith to outsource other things.

Christine: Awesome. Running a company remotely in your opinion and traveling around, there's no cons. Is there any hard parts?

Dan: Other than time zone syncing, there are no cons. If you're in Asia but your team is US-based, you have to sacrifice late night meetings sometimes. Again, when you're not in the business and you're strictly working on the business, you can set those times and prioritize the syncs to happen so that you get the most out of your team meetings. We also use Slack. It's amazing the technology that exists to let you manage a virtual team. We use Slack, and we use this really awesome service called Front, frontapp.com. It's a shared inbox solution for your whole team that lets you have conversations about email threads without actually emailing people, and you can assign emails to people.

Christine: I like it. Again, how many years have you been traveling total, do you think?

Dan: Solo, single traveling since late 2015.

Christine: Cool. What did you like least about it? What was the hardest part?

Dan: Routine or lack thereof is probably the most challenging thing that you'll run across when you live a location-independent lifestyle. If you crave routine, it's a bit of a challenge when you're hopping from city to city where you don't have the spot that you usually go to or the restaurant that you usually go to or the gym you usually go to. You need to work on your adaptability skills if you're constantly on the go. It is exciting up to a certain point. I'm at this point now where I see the benefit in staying in one city, posting up in one city indefinitely and then just traveling from there but having a home to come back to. In fact, I would recommend that for anybody that's considering this life, to have a home base and then you travel from that home base and have a place to come back to, which I never really developed that since I have family on the East Coast, friends in a bunch of different cities, a San Diego crew. I'm in New York City right now. It's worth investing in home basis because it allows you to develop that sense of home and routine that you can't necessarily get when you're traveling all the time. Same with coliving type of environments. When you're in a coliving environment, you really dial in your routine. When we were staying in the Entourage House, most of our routine was automated and we had people helping us do things like cooking and cleaning, washing the dishes. Our routines were super dialed in. That just excelled. All of our businesses grew substantially during that six-month period.

Christine: Yeah, for sure. Routine is key, and that's definitely a complaint I've heard with people that have traveled. I know me and you go a while back and the other thing you had said especially when you did the round-the-world thing was that you were like jumping cities every two weeks, right, roughly? It was hard for you. You would network. You'd meet people, but they knew you were leaving in two weeks, so it's harder to create those deep bonds with people.

Dan: It's harder to create deep connections because subconsciously, you're like, "But I'm leaving." It's hard for dating as well. It's very difficult to date if you're looking for a long-term relationship. You need to be somewhere for the long term because not everybody can mesh with that lifestyle. That's been a challenge. Overall though, it's great to have the capacity to be able to do that. You just have to find that balance that works for you.

Christine: Cool. Good stuff. What do you specifically look for when choosing a place to stay? Do you go on Airbnb? Do you look at the location? Do you look at what people you're going to live with?

Dan: First choose your city. There's a couple of good websites that let you choose good cities to post up or work from as a nomad. I think it's called Nomad List.

Christine: Nomad List. Nomad list is my favorite. I know. I'm trying so hard to create or have somebody else create something just like it for coliving. That's the one we would want to model. I love it. You go in there and then do you go in the chat section or where do you go?

Dan: I just look at the stats from each city. It'll give you stats like cities with the best Wi-Fi, best dating, best weather. Let's say you pick a city. Let's say it's Lisbon. Next step is I go to Google Maps and type in Lisbon, and then I search café. What I do is I look at the highest density of cafés in the city because generally, those are happening spots that also have coworking spaces and amazing food and nightlife and cafés to work from during the day if you're on a virtual company or places to meet for dinner or lunch. I'll find where that place is and maybe do a little Google Street View just to see if it's, oh, this is a quaint little area, and then I'll use that as the destination on Airbnb, and I'll find a spot local where all the cafés are.

Christine: I'll do that. I hope people are writing this down. Good hack. That's how you find your places. My last question for you is, what is, in your opinion, you've talked a little bit about it, what's the future of coliving? What's the future of housing as a service? You own a SaaS company. That was software as a service, and that's where you play. Do you see housing becoming a service?

Dan: 100%. I see a lot of different related trends that are all coming to a point for housing has a service. I see experience as a service. I see all these companies that are creating customized experiences, bucket list experiences, trips. These experiences platforms are becoming a thing for our generation because we like doing cool, adventurous stuff, but we don't want to necessarily plan it. I see that as a trend. I see obviously Airbnb and shared everything. There's an Uber or an Airbnb for everything. There's a new furniture company that I told you about, furnish.co, where you can rent your furniture out. There's other macro trends like coworking. Coworking is now the hippest thing you could possibly do. Companies are paying for their employees to work out of coworking spaces. There's more and more events in our world like the Freedom Fest that's happening in two weeks in Spain that I really wanted to go to, but I can't make it. All with this concept of freedom and being able to choose who you work with and who you're surrounding yourself with, especially with our generation who seek these deeper, meaningful relationships, not only in their social life but in their work life. It just all seems like it's coming together for the benefit of something like a coliving environment. I also talk to a lot of people that share the same vision I have of being able to go to a city anywhere, awesome cities all over the world, and having a community that you can immediately tap into to learn and grow and work with as well as experience a completely new city and culture. It's just the technology exists to pull this off. I'm a big proponent of the actual model because I've lived in a coliving situation, and I've experienced the benefits firsthand. I would highly suggest to look into it and giving it a shot. No matter if you're in your early 20s or if you're in your 30s or even in your 40s. It's great if you're single because it taps you into a social network, but even if you're not single, you guys can move in together and really experience and immerse yourself in a new city and have an immediate group that will not only hold you accountable but give you cool, fun things to do. I'm a big fan of it. I appreciate you, Chrissy, for championing the cause.

Christine: I'm excited to do it. I echo all your same thoughts. It'll be fun to see where things go and how fast they go because that's for sure the direction. There's no doubt about it. Well, Dan, thank you so much for your time for doing this interview. I really appreciate it.

Dan: Thanks for having me on. If anyone wants to get a hold of me, you can reach me at dan@investorfuse.com.

Interview with Chelsey Lake | Digital Developer, Marketer, Designer

Christine: Hi, everybody. Christine here again with Kindred Quarters and really excited today. We have one of the females representing, Chelsey Lake. She is a digital nomad and has been for about four years, so she's going to be sharing her story about traveling the word, how she does it, why she does, so I'm gonna let her launch right into it.

Chelsey: Okay, awesome. Little bit of backstory. I was 25. I lived in downtown Toronto in a condo like concrete jungle, very nine to five, go to an office, repeat, and I just decided, yeah, I don't wanna do that anymore and I sold my condo. I sold everything I owned, everything, and I had a Honda Fit. I loved it. It's an amazing little travel car, a rucksack, and then I got a remote job. I was already working 50% of the time remotely because I do website and development, and then I just took off three months across the country in Canada from east coast to west coast and lived out of my car, so that's how I got started.

Christine: That's a good story. Then did you just work out of coffee shops or where did you work out of?

Chelsey: Yes. Starbucks, coffee shops, anywhere that had a really good internet connection. It was my first time really ever doing it, too, so I wasn't sure where to go or who I could talk to about it, so it was very much just kind of touch and go for a while.

Christine: That was four years ago, so then fast forward. What countries have you been to now?

Chelsey: I lived in Ecuador for a while. That was one that I stayed in for a bit and Norway, too. That was my latest one which I really, really loved, but otherwise just everything. Mexico, California, British Columbia. Everything. Africa. I just like to travel, so it's been an adventure.

Christine: Then what do you love most about it?

Chelsey: The freedom, probably. I'm meeting new people. It's really, really exciting to run into other people doing the exact same work I'm doing and that's what really keeps my inspired. When I was in Ecuador, I was working with a fellow digital marketer and that's why I stayed because we kind of jammed and I got comfortable and I was like, "This is awesome."

Christine: That's super cool. You do mostly web development? What other kinds of digital marketing do you do?

Chelsey: I do funnel building mostly, so I'll do product launches. I'll build summits. I do a lot of bit of everything, so I'm very much a generalist, so design, development, launches, summits, everything.

Christine: My next question is what would you say you like least about living this type of lifestyle?

Chelsey: It might sound a little funny, but it's really, really hard to find a routine to work out, stay in shape. How do you do that when you're traveling and you don't know where to go and you don't know what's going on? Finding random gyms to stop into and getting a free day pass, that's difficult, and also meeting people. It's really hard to establish a community when you're not somewhere for a really long time, but you also really want to be around people that are like you and really spirited and excited about building things, so that can be kind of hard sometimes because it can be lonely sometimes.

Christine: Even when I've traveled, there's been times where, yeah, I'll just kind of isolate. I'll be in a beautiful country, but I'll just isolate in my hotel room for a couple days like what am I doing? Yeah, that's definitely been a common theme amongst people that are living the digital nomad life. How do you find the places you stay at?

Chelsey: That has been interesting in the beginning, because my first stint of this was in my car. After that, I Airbnbd for a while. That was my next go-to and then as I started building more networks, now I just throw it out there and I get other people coming like, "Oh, I'm gonna be in this city at this place and I'll be living in this coworking space," or, "You can stay at my parents houses in Spain because there's no one there right now," and I'm like, "Oh, perfect. Thanks." It's nice when you start building the networks, but three years ago, I wouldn't have known anybody or even know where to begin.

Christine: Then what do you look for when deciding on where? Obviously, you put it out to your networks and that's word of mouth and that's perfect, but if you're looking for Airbnb, where do you look for specifically?

Chelsey: Probably a really good internet connection. That's my go-to. Otherwise, I'm not picky at all. I kind of like the adventure of not really knowing what I'm getting myself into sometimes, I suppose.

Christine: And doing this alone and doing this as a female, I have to give you some credit for sure. I know it's more common now. I even did a road trip through the Midwest. I did a road trip last year and I think I was in Salt Lake City, Utah, or something on the way out, and people were like, "You're driving alone? You're doing a road trip alone?" I'm like, "Yeah." I don't even think twice, but that's cool, but sleeping in your car. Where would you park your car?

Chelsey: Yeah, that's a great question. My parents didn't like that one too much. In Canada, honestly, it's just so much wide open spaces everywhere. I actually slept at a lot of churches. So churches and fields, that kind of thing. I woke up surrounded by sheep one day. The only time I ever, ever got anyone interested in my car was in Jasper in Canada and I had a cop come over and be like, "Hey, what are you doing?" I was like, "Oh, I'm just taking a nap." He was like, "Okay, just making sure you're safe," and that was that, so that's the most interaction in three months I had with someone interested in why I was sleeping in my car.

Christine: Yeah, that's good. That's awesome. Oh, my gosh. Then, was there a place that you wish that you didn't wanna leave? Talk about a time where you loved where you were at and you didn't wanna actually leave, but maybe you already had the flight booked or something.

Chelsey: Yeah, definitely, definitely Norway. It was a dream. Just beautiful. Just the spirit there. They're very open and they're kind of the free spirits there. It was just really exciting and I also was working with another digital nomad the whole time, so we were traveling the whole time together getting to explore things, but also work on things, so if we went on a huge hike or something, we would talk about our projects and by the time we got back, we'd be excited to work again, so that was really, really great and I never wanted to leave. It was beautiful.

Christine: Then, what about Visa issues? Has that been hard to navigate?

Chelsey: Not really mostly because each place kind of has a set amount of time you're allowed to stay, so if I need to leave and come back, I'll just cross the border, go somewhere else, and then come right back.

Christine: Don't they call them Visa rents or something? Awesome, and then this is my last question and the most important one. What's your opinion on where this industry of coliving is going?

Chelsey: This is a super passionate subject for me because it's what I wish existed when I started and it's what I'm really excited about right now. Having other people around that you're excited to work with gets more work done faster and also it makes the whole traveling experience better because then you're surrounded with like-minded people and that's so underrated, I think, having that community that is also excited about working on the same things you're working on, so I'm really excited about that. I think our generation, too, we're about community over competition which I really, really love. We wanna work together. We wanna share all these amazing ideas and I think that's amazing, so I'm really excited about it. I can't wait. I'm gonna be an early adopter.

Christine: We have this great group called Freedom Shapers like a private little Facebook group that we're all in just about having freedom and how do we create that for ourselves and for everybody it's different, but as she reached out to me yesterday and was like,

"Hey, I would love to participate. I'm passionate about this subject," so I appreciate that. Thank you so much. I got really excited because yeah, it's the early adopters that are getting on board now and it's gonna be so exciting to see where this goes long-term and just making housing more just available. I wouldn't even say affordable. It's mostly just making it super easy, super available, flexible, right, no leases of 12 months. Like Airbnb, essentially, but the biggest disconnect is like-minded people, so you can't search on Airbnb right now of I wanna live with other people that are digital marketers or web designers, so that's where it's like, okay, how do you plug into those communities while you travel?

Chelsey: Yeah, that's exactly it. So I think it's great what you're doing because it's gonna help a lot of people like me, and I know so many other people like me that are just waiting for this. I am in Charlotte Town Rhode Island, so that's the very east coast of Canada. I'm going to be here for probably another two months, but no firm deadline.

Christine: I love it. Again, that's the freedom of being able to be like, "Okay, we're here for now, but it might change." Awesome. Chelsey, thank you again so much for doing this interview with me. I really appreciate it.

Interview with Adam Andrews | Founder of Ideal Influencers

Christine: Perfect. Hello. It's Christine here with Kindred Quarters, excited to have Adam Andrews on. He is with Ideal Influencers, and he's in Colombia now living there. But he's definitely had plenty of experience as a digital nomad, so I'm really excited to have him on today. So let's go ahead and launch right into it. Adam, do you mind telling us your story, how you got started, kind of where you've traveled to thus far?

Adam: Yeah, totally. So my digital nomad journey started off in Los Angeles in December of 2017. I was showing one of my best friends, Rob, LA for the first time. Then, when we were there we were staying at Beverly Hills, and he said, "Hey, going out to Medellín, Colombia for a month with my friend. It'll be perfect timing. You should come along." And I was like, "Nah, I'm good. No. I don't even have a passport. I'm good." I ended up looking at flight details, and ended up just booking a flight, like, 20 minutes later and told him, "Guess who's coming to Colombia with you?" And started off that journey. Booked a flight without a passport, had to expedite my passport because the flight was, like, 20 or 25 days away, so had to really get that passport expedited. Then, basically went from knowing no Spanish to knowing a little and trying to get by ordering food and whatnot in Medellín, experiencing the culture, meeting new people out here. Then we went back into the states for Las Vegas to the 10X Growth Con by Grant Cardone. Went to Portland, Oregon for a little while. Cabo San Lucas for spring break, because I'm a 20 year old college dropout and I figured, "Why not go and experience that for a little while?" Then we went to Cancun to finish off the month and kind of relax, and then came back out here for the remainder of the year.

Christine: Nice! Obviously, I mean, you went back. So you loved living down there?

Adam: Yeah, I absolutely love it. The culture is just amazing. The people out here are super nice. The food, it could use a little spice. I'm from Cali, so I love a little spice in my food. But, you know, it makes up for it. I'm learning Spanish and connecting with some awesome high-level people out here.

Christine: I love it. So obviously that's what you love most about being able to be a digital nomad and travel. Are there some things that you don't like or that are hard about it?

Adam: Yeah. So finding actually good places to live with people that are respectful is one. Airbnb, like, it helps finding places, obviously, that's why they're, like, a multibillion-dollar company. But I think finding places to live with like-minded people is hard, as well as a couple other things. But that's pretty much the majority of the issue in traveling, besides having to pack very minimalistic; finding places to live that are reasonably priced with some decent people is probably the hardest.

Christine: So you usually use Airbnb? Do you do any coliving? How often do you jump around with places?

Adam: So I'm just about six months into my digital nomad journey, so I've kind of got a feel for exactly how long I need to stay in a place to be effective and actually grow my business, and that's anywhere from, like, two to four months. If I go any less I really get distracted and overwhelmed with activities in the city, and meetups with new people and things like that, and trying to experience the city. So anything under, like, two months I kind of get distracted and don't get a lot of work done, at least effective work. But I've found that jumping around in three to four-month spans is perfect for me, because I'm able to settle in, do my activities around the city and get to know the city, as well as experience the culture, and then I also get to focus on my business. So I haven't done any coliving, mainly Airbnb and living with a couple friends. But for the most part, I'm interested in doing a coliving. There's one in Bali that I'm very interested in doing sometime next year. But for the most part, just Airbnb long-term stays.

Christine: And has there ever been a time so far that you wanted to stay in a place longer, you didn't want to leave a living situation, just because maybe you liked the area, or the place, or the people? Has that happened yet?

Adam: Yes, definitely. I absolutely loved Portland. I had two weeks to just kind of blow off. So I was like, "Screw it. I'll buy a flight from Vegas to Portland." It was cheap. And I went out to Portland for two weeks. I had been there previously for a month and absolutely fell in love with the city; fell in love with the first place that I stayed at, which was a hostel near one of the best coffee streets in the entire city, and I love coffee, so that was fantastic for me. But having to move out of there because there was only very limited living situations there was kind of a bummer. But it also had its ups and downs.

Christine: No, I've heard really good things. I know a few people that have stayed up there temporarily and they loved it. Then, so my final question and most important question is, in your personal opinion, Adam, where do you see the industry of coliving going?

Adam: Probably nothing but up, because of how Airbnb has affected the rental market and just how housing is in general, the housing markets in big cities are just ridiculously expensive. Coming from San Francisco, I can tell you rent is absolutely insane. Like, I came from San Francisco, which is like, $20,000, $25,000 a month in rent for the family, to Medellín where I can live in a penthouse with a full-time chef, a full-time maid, a doorman, and bomb-ass WiFi for less than like, $3,000 a month. So, you know, I see it expanding a lot, especially with the rental market and kind of how Airbnb has gone.

Christine: Awesome. And I agree 110% for sure. I think people want flexibility, right, and freedom? They don't want to be locked into something for 12 months.

Adam: Yep, absolutely. Yeah, that's a huge part of it, too. I was looking at living in Portland and I was going to live out there for like three months. But an Airbnb out there is just, like, ridiculous. I mean, not compared to San Francisco, but just on the budget that I was trying to keep myself accountable towards and the budget I had set for the business. I was trying to keep under that budget, and it just wasn't making sense. And people wanted me to sign leases and check my credit, and I was like, "I just want to live in this place for a little while. Why can't I just do that?" And hostels don't work, and hotels are too expensive. So, yeah, I see coliving definitely as a market to be expanding in quite a bit. There's a lot of growth.

Christine: Awesome! Well, thank you so much again, Adam, for taking the time to speak with us on this interview. Again, it's nice to get the leaders of the coliving industry and the founders, and then also the people that were actually digital nomads, and they're using the spaces and they're traveling the world. So it's nice to have the different perspectives. Thank you so much!

Adam: Awesome. Thank you as well. Let me know also how I can possibly invest. I'm interested in investing in this coliving marketspace.

Afterword

August 6, 2018

I am so excited that this book that I've been dreaming of is finally real.

Hopefully you can tell how passionate I am about coliving and why it's such an exciting time. These interviews were an amazing way to talk with fellow leaders in the space and really inject some new perspectives as well as reinforce so many concepts emphasized in the book. Their messages really resonated with me, as I'm hoping they did with you too. It was so refreshing to hear the variety of innovation on a global level, and the degree of mastery that these individuals have been able to reach in their unique domains. Each of them brings something new and valuable to the table.

So, now that you know all of this incredibly valuable information about the industry and how to approach it, where do we go from here? I want to share my visions for the future with you so we can imagine how to advance forward. One way that I see this going is toward greater accessibility and ease with tech catching up to complement it. For example, I look forward to seeing apps and services develop, such as an online directory which can link people to amazing coliving spaces across the world in a matter of seconds.

Although we have plenty of housing services now which help people find living arrangements, they have not yet tapped into the interactive aspect regarding who guests will actually be living with. Other services help to link roommates but do not provide the housing aspect. Hopefully we can bring these together! This is where I hope to see (or create) some change, where people can use their phone to book a room on the App with like-minded others. The ability to travel to a new location and know that new friends await who share your mindset is a much-needed shakeup in the field. This new movement of HaaS (housing as a service) is reinventing what it means to be home. With these changes, anywhere across the world can feel like home, even if it's a new place thousands of miles away. This is what I'm so excited about—no more isolation, loneliness, or fear of exploration. Instead, people can embrace the full extent of their aspirations knowing that they will always feel a sense of home wherever they are.

With all of these amazing shifts, my greatest hope is that I can help and inspire people to succeed on this journey too. I'm in the process of expanding my company, Kindred Quarters, to provide even more accessibility to these spaces in additional key cities. However, if this book ends up helping you, whether you go on to move in a coliving home, invest in one, or create your own, I am honored to be a part of your journey in any way. And in the end, that's what coliving is all about—supporting one another to help them succeed and knowing that uplifting others does the same to yourself.